SOCIAL PROBLEMS
AND
SOCIAL POLICY:
The American Experience

This is a volume in the Arno Press Series

SOCIAL PROBLEMS
AND
SOCIAL POLICY:
The American Experience

Advisory Editor
Gerald N. Grob

Editorial Board
Clarke A. Chambers
Blanche D. Coll
Walter I. Trattner

See last pages of this volume
for a complete list of titles.

OPIUM-SMOKING

IN

AMERICA AND CHINA

H[arry] H[ubbell] Kane

1551330

ARNO PRESS

A New York Times Company

New York — 1976

Editorial Supervision: SHEILA MEHLMAN

———◆———

Reprint Edition 1976 by Arno Press Inc.

Reprinted from a copy in the Theological Seminary of
  New Brunswick Library

SOCIAL PROBLEMS AND SOCIAL POLICY: The American Experience
ISBN for complete set: 0-405-07474-3
See last pages of this volume for titles.

Manufactured in the United States of America

———◆———

Library of Congress Cataloging in Publication Data

Kane, Harry Hubbell, 1854–
    Opium-smoking in America and China.

    (Social problems and social policy—the American
experience)
    Reprint of the ed. published by Putnam, New York.
    Bibliography: p.
    1. Opium habit. I. Title. II. Series.
RC568.06K36 1976   616.8'63   75-17227
ISBN 0-405-07497-2

OPIUM-SMOKING

IN

AMERICA AND CHINA

A STUDY OF ITS PREVALENCE, AND EFFECTS, IMME-
DIATE AND REMOTE, ON THE INDIVIDUAL
AND THE NATION

BY

H. H. KANE, M.D.

AUTHOR OF "THE HYPODERMIC INJECTION OF MORPHIA: ITS HISTORY, ADVAN-
TAGES, AND DANGERS;" AND "DRUGS THAT ENSLAVE: A STUDY OF THE
OPIUM, MORPHINE, CHLORAL, AND HASHISCH HABITS"

"That leads to bewilder, and dazzles to blind."

"Pleasures, hopes, affections gone.
    The wretch must bear and yet live on."

———

NEW YORK
G. P. PUTNAM'S SONS
27 & 29 WEST 23D STREET
1882

Press of
G. P. Putnam's Sons
New York

PREFACE.

IN my work, " Drugs That Enslave," which is devoted to a study of the opium, morphine,
chloral, and hashisch habits, I say, at p. 29, that
opium-smoking is confined entirely to the inhabitants
of Eastern countries, and that, consequently, a
study of the subject can in no way interest us.
This statement, in the light of my present knowledge, is wholly false, as also is an accompanying
clause in which I say that a full description of the
practice may be found in books of travel. The descriptions there found are either very meagre, and
consequently worthless, or positively untruthful.

That opium-smoking is a vice that imperatively
demands careful study at the hands of Americans is made manifest by the fact that the practice,
comparatively unknown amongst us six years ago,
is now indulged in by some six thousand of our
countrymen, male and female, whose ranks are being daily recruited from the over-curious, foolish,
indolent, or wilfully vicious; that large and small
towns in the West, and large cities in the East
abound in places where this drug is sold and

smoked ; and that in some of our States it has been
found necessary to enact laws imposing a heavy
money penalty and imprisonment upon the seller
and the smoker.

My attention was first called to this matter, prac-
tically, by the advent of a smoker at my Home for
treatment. About thirty-five years of age, thoroughly educated, of marked conversational powers,
and having travelled in many countries, he told me
of things relating to the practice of this vice by
Americans that at first excited my incredulity.
Upon actual demonstration in this city, however,
incredulity gave place to astonishment and full belief, and I at once set myself to the task of obtaining full and authentic information upon the
subject.

I did not rely alone upon the statements made to
me by this gentleman, but wrote to those chiefs of
police, physicians, and public men in various parts
of the country who would be likely to know something about the matter. Much, too, was gathered
from two smokers whom I subsequently had under
treatment, and a number of the American smokers,
male and female, in this city, and some from California and Nevada, who have kindly come to my
house to smoke, thus affording me unusual facilities
for studying the effects of the drug, when thus used,
on different indi iduals and upon the various sys-

tems, organs, and apparatuses of each. These persons have been seen smoking, at various times, either at my house or at the dens, and have been freely interrogated upon most of the points upon which I am about to dwell by Drs. E. C. Spitzka, N. S. Westcott, Thomas Skinner, G. H. Wynkoop, Chas. E. Locke, Stephen W. Roof, Thos. Brennan, and F. Pinner, of New York City; Dr. John Papin, of St. Louis; Mr. J. A. Alexander and F. de Thulstrup, artists for Harper Bros.; Mr. E. P. Roe, of Cornwall-on-the-Hudson; Mr. Schœnduv, of the *N. Y. Tribune*, Jos. Lawrence, of this city, Mr. Gilder, editor of *Scribner's Monthly*, and some members of the art department of the same journals, also some others whose names I cannot now recall, all of whom can vouch for the accuracy of many of the statements I am about to make regarding the manner of smoking and the immediate effects of the indulgence.

Two of my male nurses very kindly obliged me by smoking the drug a number of times, thus affording me special facilities for study, as they were constantly under my observation, and I was able to note more closely and accurately both the immediate and remote effects upon the novice. Finally, I smoked myself a number of times, both in large and small amounts, and often to decided excess, so that I might be the better able to fully understand the subjective symptoms. Otherwise I should have

been obliged to depend upon the word of the habitual smoker, which is not always reliable.

It was my intention at first to confine what I had
to say to the practice of this vice amongst Americans, but the importance of the question of the
Anglo-Oriental opium trade, with the interest it is
now exciting in both England and China, led me to
add a chapter upon that aspect of the subject. In
this connection I cannot too heartily commend the
stand taken by, and the noble efforts of, the Anglo-
Oriental Society for the Suppression of the Opium
Trade. While I cannot agree with every thing that
is maintained by that body of earnest and honest
workers, I do so in the main. Upon certain medical
points I believe the testimony of laymen, either
English or Chinese, to be wholly worthless, and I
hold that with regard to certain questions there has
been too great readiness to accept all evils happen-
ing to the Chinese individual, or nation, as the certain result of indulgence in this vice. Statistics are
too meagre, and too many factors enter into the
problem to make it appear as simple as some would
have us believe. From whatever side we view it,
however, the responsibility of the English government in fostering and forcing this vice upon the
Chinese people, finds no justification, and continuance of the trade at the present day merits only
condemnation.

To the following gentlemen I find myself deeply indebted for facts givèn, reference to bibliography, or assistance in my search: Drs. G. B. Harris, of Virginia City, Nevada; G. Shurtleff, of the State Insane Asylum, Stockton, California, and P. C. Remondino, Health Officer, San Diego, Cal.; Mr. D. C. Robbins, of the firm of McKesson & Robbins, this city; Joseph Nimmo, Esq., of the Bureau of Statistics, Treasury Department, Washington, D. C.; the gentlemen of the State Department at Washington; Mr. John Wallace, of Chicago, Ill.; Frederick Kimball, of New York; George D. Dowkorett, of the N. Y. Medical Mission; Frederick Wells Williams, son of S. Wells Williams, the eminent scholar and author of "The Middle Kingdom" Mr. Tom Lee, Chinese deputy sheriff, this city; Ah Sing, keeper of a "joint" in Mott Street; Senator Jones, of Nevada; and Dr. William Simpson, of San Jose, California.

The following is a list of the works consulted in obtaining facts relative to this subject:

WILLIAMS, S. WELLS. The Middle Kingdom; a survey of the geography, government, education, social life, arts, religion, etc., of the Chinese Empire and its inhabitants. N, Y., 1879.

ANDREWS. India and her Neighbors. N. Y., 1878.

SHUCK, J. LEWIS. Portfolio Chinensis; a collection of authentic Chinese State papers. Macao, China, 1840.

CALKINS, ALONZO. Opium and the Opium Appetite. Phila., 1871.

MACFARLANE, CHAS. The Chinese Revolution, with details of the habits, manners, and customs of China and the Chinese. London, 1853.

United States Consular Reports from 1870 to 1881.

LEVENSTEIN, EDWARD. Morbid Craving for Morphia. London, 1878.

HUC, Abbé M. Travels in China. N. Y., 1855.

———— Travels in Tartary and Thibet.

The Opium Habit, with suggestions as to remedy. N. Y., 1868.

DAVIS, JOHN FRANCIS. The Chinese. London, 1836.

ALLEN, NATHAN. The Opium Trade. Lowell, 1853.

British Medical Journal, 1867.

COOKE. The Seven Sisters of Sleep, 1869.

GUTZLAFF. Junk Voyage Along the Coast of China.

Singapore Free Press, June 13, 1839.

BOWRING, Sir JOHN. The Kingdom and People of Siam. London, 1857.

Chinese Repository, vols. 1 to 20 inclusive.

BURNES. Travels into Bokhara, 1834.

Merchants' Magazine, vol. 23, pp. 28 and 146.

PALGRAVE, W. G. Central and Eastern Arabia. London, 1873.

FLÜCKIGER and HANBURY. Pharmacographia : a history of drugs. London, 1879.

SEWARD, GEO. F. Chinese Immigration in its Social and Economical Aspects. N. Y., 1880.

RICHARDSON, B. W. Diseases of Modern Life. N. Y., 1878.

SPEER, WILLIAM. China and the United States. Hartford, 1870.

MEDHURST, W. H. The Foreigner in Far Cathay.

MEDHURST, W. H. China, its State and Prospects. Boston, 1838.

The Nemesis in China.

MARTIN, ———. China.

JOCELYN, Lord. Six Months with the Chinese Expedition. London, 1841.

India, Pictorial, Historical, and Descriptive.

ALCOCK, Sir RUTHERFORD. China and its Foreign Relations. Article in *Contemporary Review*, December, 1880.

KNOX, THOS. W. John ; or, Our Chinese Relations. Harper Brós. Half-Hour Series.

OLIPHANT. China and Japan.

DOOLITTLE. Travels in China.

ATKINSON. Amoor Regions.

LJANSTADT, Sir ANDREW. Historical Sketch of Portuguese Settlements in China.

McPHERSON, Dr. D. Two Years in China. London, 1843.

The Argosy, Aug., 1866, p. 161, article, ' My Chinese Neighbors " in Australia.

ALLOM and WRIGHT. Pictorial History of the Chinese. London, 1853.

ALLEN, D. O. India, Ancient and Modern. Boston, 1856.

Appleton's Encyclopædia.

Encyclopædia Britannica.

Chambers's Encyclopædia.

COOLEY. Handbook of Practical Receipts.

The Rupture with China and its Causes ; a letter to Lord Palmerston by a resident in China. London, 1840.

FRY, Sir EDWARD. England, China, and Opium : three essays reprinted from the *Contemporary Review*.

MOULE, ARTHUR, E., B.D.   The Opium Question ; a review of the opium policy of Great Britain and its results to India and China.

TINLING, J. F. B., B.A.   The Poppy Plague and England's Crime.

TURNER, F. S., B.A.   British Opium Policy and its Results to India and China.

CHALMERS, J., D.D.   Reply of the K'Euen Keae Shay, the Canton Association for the Promotion of Abstinence from Opium, to the Address of the Anglo-Oriental Society for the Suppression of the Opium Trade.   Translated from the Chinese.

The Friend of China, published once in two months.

Sir William Muir's Minute, and other extracts from papers published by the Calcutta Government.

MANDER, SAMUEL S.   Our Opium Trade with China.   With appendix.   Fifth thousand.

Our National Responsibility for the Opium Trade.   A sketch prepared for the use of Members of, and Candidates for, Parliament.

Report of the Debate in the House of Commons on the Motion of J. W. Pease, Esq., M.P., June 4, 1880.

McCARTHY, JUSTIN.   The Opium War.

England and the Opium Trade with China.

DAVIES, J. LLEWELYN, M.A.   International Christianity.   Reprinted from the *Contemporary Review.*

The Opium Monopoly.

The Opium-Smoker.

FOWLER, R. N., M.A., F.R.G.S., M.P.   The Opium Revenue of India.

Appeal to the Clergy.

What the Chinese think about Opium.

ORMEROD W. E.   Our Opium Trade with China, and England's Injustice toward the Chinese.

Alcohol and Opium.

Our National Opium Trade : its character and effects described by extracts from Blue-books.   Sixteen pages.

The Facts of the Opium Trade.

Fourth and Fifth Annual Reports of the Society for the Suppression of the Opium Trade, 1880, 1881.

Publications of the Anglo-Oriental Society for the Suppression of the Opium Trade.

THELWALL.   Iniquities of the Opium Trade with China.   London, 1853.

POQUEVILLE.   Travels in Morea.

CHRISTLIEB, THEO., D.D., Ph.D.   The Indo-British Opium Trade.

I must acknowledge my indebtedness to Mr. William Wood, of 27 Great Jones Street, for the use of the electrotypes of the pipe and lay-out that appear at pp. 33 and 36.   They appeared originally with my article in the *N. Y. Medical Record*, of Nov. 5, 1881, entitled " The Chinese Opium Pipe as a Therapeutic Agent."   Also to Mr. John Wiley for the use of the cut representing opium-smoking in China, taken from S. Wells Williams' " Middle Kingdom."

THE DE QUINCY HOME,
          Fort Washington, New York City.

CONTENTS.

SYNOPSIS BY CHAPTERS.

CHAPTER VI.

CHAPTER VII.

CHAPTER VIII.

OPIUM SMOKING IN AMERICA AND CHINA.

CHAPTER I.

Origin and spread of the vice in America.—The class who smoke.—
Laws of California and Nevada.—Statistics of import and of
Chinese population.—Amount smoked.

THE first white man who smoked opium in
America is said to have been a sporting character, named Clendenyn. This was in California, in
1868. The second—induced to try it by the first—
smoked in 1871. The practice spread rapidly and
quietly among this class of gamblers and prostitutes
until the latter part of 1875, at which time the
authorities became cognizant of the fact, and finding, upon investigation, that many women and
young girls, as also young men of respectable family,
were being induced to visit the dens, where they
were ruined morally and otherwise, a city ordinance
was passed forbidding the practice under penalty of
a heavy fine or imprisonment, or both. Many arrests
were made, and the punishment was prompt and
thorough.

On this account the vice was indulged in much less openly, but none the less extensively, for although the larger smoking-houses were closed, the small dens in Chinatown were well patronized, and the vice grew surely and steadily.

The very fact that opium-smoking was a practice forbidden by law seemed to lead many who would not otherwise have indulged to seek out the low dens and patronize them, while the regular smokers found additional pleasure in continuing that about which there was a spice of danger. It seemed to add zest to their enjoyment. Men and women, young girls,—virtuous or just commencing a downward career,—hardened prostitutes, representatives of the "hoodlum" element, young clerks and errand-boys who could ill afford the waste of time and money, and young men who had no work to do, were to be found smoking together in the back rooms of laundries in the low, pestilential dens of Chinatown, reeking with filth and overrun with vermin, in the cellars of drinking-saloons and in houses of prostitution. No one can question the fascination of a vice, the strength of a habit that will lead people into such degradation for the gratification of the abnormal appetite. No one can question the certainty of moral ruin, the charring and obliteration of every honest impulse and honorable sentiment, the sweeping away of every vest-

ment of modesty, by such associations and such surroundings. It needs no sign-board to mark the
terminus of this road.

Dr. Harris, of Virginia City, Nevada, in answer
to a letter of inquiry, says:

Opium-smoking had been entirely confined to the Chinese up to
and before the autumn of 1876, when the practice was introduced by
a sporting character who had lived in China, where he had contracted
the habit. He spread the practice amongst his class, and his mistress,
" a woman of the town," introduced it among her *demi-monde*
acquaintances, and it was not long before it had widely spread
amongst the people mentioned, and then amongst the younger class
of boys and girls, many of the latter of the more respected class of
families. The habit grew very rapidly, until it reached young
women of more mature age, when the necessity for stringent measures became apparent, and was met by the passing of a city ordinance.

This attempt at prohibition was a failure, and finally the Legislature passed a very stringent law making the penalty imprisonment.
At our last Legislature a law was passed making the punishment a
penitentiary one, and by the vigilance of the officers the crime is on
the decrease, or, at least, the evil habit is checked. The law not
only reaches the *smokers*, but any one *keeping* a den where those
smokers resort, as well as *holding the premises* responsible. The law
goes so far as to make it a crime for any person to be found with
opium on his person unless prescribed by a physician. I have made
every inquiry, and through our Chief of Police, J. Bradley, I find
that the habit is getting down to " cappers " of gambling-houses and
the lower classes.

Had it not been for this last stringent law, whereby the authorities
make descents upon any place where suspicion rests, I am satisfied
that the habit would have extended into the higher classes, as the
practice and habit are quickly acquired.

In California the law is less stringent.   Any person using it, or found with a pipe and opium, is fined $50 for the first offense, and for the second $500 and six months in County Jail.

Dr. G. A. Shurtleff, Superintendent of the State Insane Asylum at Stockton, Cal., and to whom I am indebted for a great deal of information, writes me :

The laws for the suppression of this vice were municipal ordinances, I think, until last winter, when the Legislature added a new section to the penal code bf the State, which is as follows :

Section 307.—"Every person who opens or maintains, to be resorted to by other persons, any place where opium, or any of its preparations, is sold or given away to be smoked at such place ; and any person who, at such place, sells or gives away any opium or its said preparations to be there smoked or otherwise used ; and every person who visits or resorts to any such place for the purpose of smoking opium or its said preparations, is guilty of a misdemeanor, and upon conviction thereof shall be punished by a fine not exceeding five hundred dollars, or by imprisonment in the County Jail not exceeding six months, or by both such fine and imprisonment."—Stat. Cal., p. 34, 1881.

The vice was not long confined to these two places. It was soon found that smokers coming East were constantly making converts, so that in a few months' time small and large towns like Truckee, Carson, Reno, and many others, each had their smoking dens and their regular customers.   Each new convert seemed to take a morbid delight in converting others, and thus the standing army was daily swelled by recruits.

In the latter part of 1876 Chicago, St. Louis, and
New Orleans fell into line, and the practice spread
with great rapidity, both in these places and to
other cities. A few months later the practice was
commenced in New York City, by three habitués.
To-day there are many places for smoking and at
least three hundred smokers here. The principal
places, known as "opium joints," are in Mott, Pell,
and Park streets, right in the centre of the Chinese
quarter. The streets are filthy, and swarm with
Chinamen, Malays, half-breeds, and a mixed tenement-house population. The houses are chiefly low
wooden structures in a dilapidated condition ; most
of them bearing upon their fronts banners or signs
marked with Chinese hieroglyphics. On the first
floor and in the basement the shrewd Chinese
merchant displays his strange-shaped and many-col-
ored wares.

My first visit to these places was made in the company of an old smoker, one dark night about 9 P. M.
Mott Street was alive with swarthy-faced Celestials
standing or sitting in front of the stores or houses,
moving noiselessly about in their thick felt-soled
shoes, or leaning from the windows of their lodge-
rooms and restaurants. Some were quietly smoking
the small tobacco pipe in which many Americans
suppose that opium is smoked; others were wildly
gesticulating and conversing in their peculiar sing-

song language; while still others, in response to the hoarse tone of a gong which announced that the game was open, filed into a gambling-saloon near by.

Descending a few steps into the basement of one of the houses we came upon a small open space containing a table, a chair, a stool, and a stove of peculiar pattern. Before us were two small square rooms boarded in. Through a curtain in a casementless window, in the small room to the left, could be seen a crowd of excited Chinamen clustered about a high table covered with matting. The light of the single kerosene lamp shining upon their swarthy faces, showed all eyes fixed upon a Chinaman who was deftly manipulating some metal pieces. They were playing a game of chance known as *fan tan* or *tan*. "The keeper of the table is provided with a pile of bright coin, of which he takes a double handful, and lays them on the table, covering them with a bowl. The persons standing outside the rail guess the remainder there will be left after the pile has been divided by four, whether 1, 2, 3, or nothing, the guess and stake of each person being first recorded by a clerk; the keeper then carefully picks out the coins, four by four, all narrowly watching his movements. Cheating is almost impossible in this game, and twenty people can play at it as easily as two." [1]

---

[1] Williams: The Middle Kingdom, vol. ii, p. 89.

The little room on the right was boarded about half way up the front, from which point small wooden bars ran to the ceiling, thus separating it from the small anteroom. Behind the bars stood a pleasant-faced Chinaman who, with scales in hand, was weighing out some opium. Inside, by the dim light, could be seen a single wooden bunk covered with matting, upon which a Chinaman was engaged in smoking opium. Going along a narrow passage that ran between the two rooms we came upon a small pillared altar before which a light and some sweet smelling pastils were burning. Swerving to the right we passed through a low doorway and found ourselves in the smoking-room.

In a few moments, after our eyes had become accustomed to the semi-gloom, we found ourselves in a small low-ceilinged room made of rough boards, about the three sides of which ran low wooden bunks some four feet in width. In the back part of the room there were two tiers of bunks. Close to the ceiling was a narrow grated window, the only means of ventilation. Upon these bunks were stretched transversely, in parties of two or three, some twelve men and women—Americans—engaged in cooking and smoking opium. The whole place was rank with the odor of the drug.

The recumbent forms, the quiet faces half lit by the little opium lamps, the subdued conversation,

the sizzing and bubbling of the pipes, served to
impress us with astonishment, and suggested something uncanny.

This place was the type of many others that we
visited. Here it is, however, that most of the
Americans smoke, and from one to twenty may be
found here during the afternoon, night, and until
early the next morning. Besides these joints, there
are others in Second and Fourth avenues, and
one in Twenty-third street, presided over by an
American woman and her two daughters. A few
Americans smoke in the back rooms of Chinese
laundries, while others, providing themselves with a
full outfit smoke together in private rooms.

In San Francisco, a woman well-known to the
police and to the sporting fraternity, located first
on Bush and then on Market street, kept a house,
the lower part of which was devoted to opium-
smoking, while the rest was let out as furnished
rooms to transient guests. Many females are so
much excited sexually by the smoking of opium
during the first few weeks, that old smokers with
the sole object of ruining them have taught them to
smoke. Many innocent and over-curious girls have
thus been seduced.

At the present day almost every town of any
note in the United States, and more especially those
in the West have their smoking dens and habitués.

Even the little frontier towns and mining camps have their layouts and their devotees. Arrests are being constantly made in San Francisco, Virginia City, New Orleans, and occasionally in Chicago. The following newspaper clippings from the *Stockton Independence*, of August 2, 1881, were sent me by Dr. G. A. Shurtleff, Superintendant of the State Insane Asylum, at Stockton, California.

POLICE COURT.

In the Police Court yesterday J. K. Simpson, Patrick Timmons, Thomas Finn, and Taylor Snyder pleaded guilty to drunkenness, and were sent up five days each in default of $5 apiece. Joseph Howe was fined a like amount, and given till four o'clock to skip. Besides these fines were imposed : Otto Myrrick, drunk, $5 ; same, disturbing the peace, $10 ; David Smith, drunk, $5 ; George Orr, drunk, five days. Harry Block and Austin Vance, drunk, forfeited $5 each. (H. H. Weber forfeited $40, and Maud McCleary, Mrs. Rogers, and Wan Hing, $20 each, for opium-smoking.) John Morgan forfeited $10 by not answering the charge of disturbing the peace. Collections yesterday, $125.

RAID ON AN OPIUM DEN.

Monday morning at 1 o'clock officers Cohen, Collins, Hornage, and Edwards raided an opium den located in a wooden building back of a house of ill fame on Market Street, between El Dorado and Hunter streets, and captured four smokers—a white man, a Chinaman, and two white women—all stretched out on bunks and enjoying a quiet smoke. The officers also captured the outfit, which consisted of four pipe bowls, one pipe stem, a small opium lamp and several boxes of opium.

ONE MAN ARRESTS TWENTY.

Officer Chris. B. Ryer, of Oakdale, Monday night, raided an opium den kept by a Chinaman named Tuck Tye, who is a merchant in that thriving village. The officer, single-handed and alone, arrested two white men and eighteen Chinamen, and locked the whole party in a room over which he stood guard all night. They will be tried before C. S. S. Hill, Esquire, Justice of the Peace of Oakdale.

I am told that in April of last year a petition signed by many of the residents of Hot Springs, Arkansas, was sent to the new chief of police, urging him to take stringent measures to close the opium-smoking dens in that place. In September of the same year a police raid in Chicago resulted in the arrest and fining of a large number of male and female smokers. In July of this year the police of this city raided a low dive in Park Street, and arrested a number of white girls who were smoking with Chinamen.

The following clipping from the *San Francisco Chronicle* of July 25, 1881, kindly sent me by Dr. P. C. Remondino, shows very well the state of things there existing despite the making and carrying out of laws against the practice.

"We don't pretend to have broken up the habit of opium-smoking," said Police-Officer James Mahoney, who has figured extensively in the raids on Chinese opium and gambling dens. "That can't be done by any number of ordinances, no matter how rigidly enforced. We have, however, closed up the opium dens. I mean by that, the places formerly kept by Chinese in Chinatown, where any one could go and smoke opium by paying for the privilege. These places were supported principally by the patronage of white men and women. The likely chance of having to pay $20 in the Police Court for the privilege has made the white smokers find other means of hitting the pipe."

"What means have they found?"

"All of them who can afford it now have their own lay-outs for smoking in their sleeping-rooms. Those who are too poor for that beg the privilege from more lucky friends. We can keep pretty good track of the number of these lay-outs around town by the number of whites who come into Chinatown for opium."

"How many rooms where opium is smoked do you suppose there are outside of Chinatown?"

"The number probably would not fall under 200. You see we can do nothing to prevent it. A man can do pretty much what he likes in his own room. Some of these rooms, south of Market Street, have been raided, but the arresting officers could not prove that they were maintained as places where opium could be smoked by any one for a consideration, and the cases were dismissed."

"Where are those rooms situated?"

"In all of the large down-town lodging-houses ; on Kearney and Stockton streets, and south of Market, on Third, Fourth, Fifth, and Sixth streets.

"Do you think the habit will gradually die out, now that you have driven the white smokers out of Chinatown?"

"Not much. It will rapidly increase. The habit in past years, so far as whites were concerned, was confined to hoodlums and prostitutes mostly. Few decent men or women would care to come into Chinatown and smoke in the filthy dens here. Now that there are scores of places where the habit can be contracted in clean rooms and in respectable portions of the city, the practice will gradually extend up the social grade. Schoolboys and clerks who would never have gone into a Chinese den are already finding out the respectable places and learning to like the habit. Of course there are a few men, otherwise respectable, who contracted the habit in Chinatown and are such slaves to the vice that they still prowl around here. I know of instances where the habit has so debased men that they prefer to smoke in the lowest and filthiest dens here. A couple of months ago we raided a den in the lower end of town and found among the white smokers a letter-carrier, whose route included a portion of Chinatown. He had become acquainted with the keepers of dens, had been asked to take a smoke, did so out of curiosity, and is now a confirmed smoker. When we arrested him he gave a fictitious name and went out on $20 bail, which he forfeited. You know that there are some men who stand very high in the community who sometimes lose their balance and go on howling drunks.

"It's nine chances to ten that if they are men moving in good society, they will wind up in the lowest dives on the Barbary Coast, where they drink the vilest whiskey they can get until they can be safely packed in a carriage and taken in charge by their friends. It's part of the disease to want to get way down in the mud, and it's the same with some opium smokers. It may sound strange, but I have had men who could easily buy their own outfit and the purest opium tell me that when the longing comes on them they cannot satisfy it except in a low Chinese den ; that the idea of smoking good opium in a clean pipe and in their own rooms don't seem to fill the bill."

The reporter accompanied the officer in a visit to some of the most noted opium dens. On Bartlett Alley, in a low, black, foul-smelling, cave-like hole underneath the sidewalk, a den was visited where thirteen Chinamen and three white boys had been arrested during the enforcement of the ordinance. It was 2 o'clock in the afternoon, and the den was occupied by six Chinese thieves, all asleep save one, who was half stupefied with the fumes from the pipe to which his swollen, nerveless lips were glued. The officer lit several lamps which form part of a smoking lay-out, and one of which was placed near each sleeper's head. By the smoking, red light thus obtained the reporter saw that most of the shelves in the den whereon white smokers erstwhile sought dreamy oblivion showed evidences of not having been used for weeks. Some of the smokers awoke, stared vacantly at the officer, and proceeded to dress or prepare again the pipe whose fumes hours ago had made them senseless. All of the dens, whose white patrons the vigilant officers have driven away, are now occupied by the lowest class of Chinese sneak thieves.

It is the class whose members prowl around back yards late at night, and steal such unguarded articles as will suffice, in trade with receivers of stolen goods, to give them funds for one day's opium and food. Ten cents will do that. Dirty, vicious, and debased, they pass their nights in stealing, their mornings in smoking, their afternoons in sleep. The white boys arrested in the Bartlett Alley den said they were "supers" in the Adelphi Theatre. They had contracted the habit, and not having money enough to purchase a lay-out had run the desperate chance of going to jail in spending their last ten-cent piece for a smoke. In a den on Jackson Street the reporter saw the system of signalling the inmates at night in case of the approach of officers. The den is still patronized late at night, the officers think, by white men and women, but it is next to impossible to surprise them in the act of smoking, which is necessary in order to secure a conviction. There appeared to be at least half a dozen means of entrance, from as many different stairways and halls. Each door leading into the den was to all appearances from the outside a solid part of the surrounding walls. The place was dark and deserted when the officer and the reporter entered. Striking a light the officer showed a string leading through a gimlet-hole in the wall and running out to one of the street entrances. On the end of the string inside the den was tied a chip, dangling upon some loose newspapers. The string, pulled from the outside of the entrance, rattles the chip on the dry papers. The warning given, the smokers had time to hustle out of any of the many exits, and the raiding officers found nothing.

In another den visited in the building on the corner of Bull Run Alley and Pacific Street the officer told the following story : Pointing to an opium-smoker's bunk, he said, "You see the space underneath that bunk there ? Well, one night some officers were informed that a white man was smoking in that den. One of the officers had with him a little rat terrier, which made itself useful in scenting out drunks in hallways. The den was approached, admittance was refused, the door was broken open, and one lone and indignant Chinaman was found inside. ' Seek them out, Scotchy,' said the officer to his dog. The dog dived under the bunk, snuffed all about the place, and came back to its master with tail dragging. The officer had such confidence in his dog that he gave up the search and went away. Afterward I learned the sequel from the white man who was under the bunk all the time. He told me that the dog came under the bunk, snuffed him, ran its cold nose into his face, and went back without a single bark. The dog, by the way, always barked like a house a-fire when he discovered a drunk or tramp. Now the question with me is whether the dog was stupefied with the fumes of the opium, or so disgusted with the smoker that he did not give the alarm."

The result of the afternoon with the intelligent officer was a conviction that Chinatown had indeed been cleared of white opium smokers. But in reaching such a conclusion a close observer is somehow constantly reminded of our advanced and highly progressive system of street-sweeping. Citizens who have been on Kearny Street late at night have noticed, possibly, a ponderous, heavy, and lumbering machine, drawn by four horses, which rattles over the street and carefully sweeps all of the dirt into nice little potato-hill-like rows. After it comes another creaking machine, drawn by six horses, which, with great precision, scatters and spatters all of the dirt all over the street again. The anti-opium-smoking ordinance drove the white smokers out of Chinatown, but the vice came along and scattered the smokers, planting them, in fact, in every portion of the city.

It is thus seen how fascinating a habit that of opium-smoking is, and with what rapidity it is spreading all over the country, ensnaring individuals in all classes of society, leading to the downfall of innocent girls and the debasement of married women, and spreading its roots and growing in spite of the most stringent measures looking to its eradication.

If this practice is as rapidly spreading in this country as we are led to believe, we should find a corresponding increase in the amount of opium imported. Fortunately for our purpose, the heavy duty—$6.00 per pound—levied on smoking-opium permits of our differentiating it, in the Treasury returns, from ordinary opium on which the duty is but $1.00 per pound. That the yearly importation is in direct ratio to the yearly demand in this country, seems almost certain from the fact that the Chinese merchants, by whom the trade is exclusively carried on, do not buy up and store away or flood the market with large quantities for purposes of speculation, and that all the opium of this kind is used up here, none leaving our ports for other countries. Such, at least, is the official statement made by the inspectors of the ports of New York and San Francisco to Joseph Nimmo, Esq., Chief of the Bureau of Statistics, Treasury Department, Washington. This gentleman has, furthermore, kindly favored me with the following table of the importation of the two forms of opium into the United States during the years from 1871 to 1880, inclusive. (See p. 16.)

From this table it will be seen that the increase in the amount of smoking-opium in the last few years has been steady, with an advance of 17,000 pounds in 1880 over that imported in 1879. The total of 77,196.00 pounds, with a money value of

Fiscal Year ended June 30.	GUM OPIUM.				OPIUM PREPARED FOR SMOKING.			
	Pounds.	Values.	Rate of Duty.	Am't of Duty.	Pounds.	Values.	Rate of Duty.	Am't of Duty.
1871 {	52,929.25	$344,683.00	$2.50 per lb.	$132,323.13	12,554.00 {	$13,635.00	100 per cent.	$13,635.00
	105,689.31	574,291.00	1.00	105,689.31	25,270.60	239,699.00	$6.00 per lb.	151,623.63
1872	189,354.50	769,750.00	"	189,354.50	49,375.00	535,596.52	"	296,250.00
1873	152,770.38	734,797.00	"	142,770.38	53,059.00	581,656.20	"	318,354.00
1874	170,706.02	945,232.00	"	170,706.02	55,343.75	556,844.00	"	232,062.50
1875	188,238.75	953,429.00	"	188,238.75	62,774.66	662,066.00	"	376,647.93
1876	228,742.28	913,078.00	"	228,742.28	53,189.42	577,288.51	"	349,136.50
1877	230,132.09	997,692.00	"	239,102.09	47,427.94	502,662.27	"	284,567.70
1878	207,752.24	712,624.00	"	207,752.24	54,804.78	617,160.20	"	328,828.65
1879	278,553.90	929,894.00	"	278,553.90	60,647.67	643,774.00	"	363,886.02
1880	243,211.31	858,225.25	"	243,211.31	77,196.00	773,796.00	"	463,176.00

about two thirds of a million dollars, of a drug used wholly in pandering to a morbid appetite (for not a single grain is used as medicine), is enormous and startling.

But stay! Cannot this increase be accounted for on the ground of a rapid increase in our Chinese population, about twenty per cent. of whom smoke opium occasionally, and fifteen per cent. smoke it daily?

From the carefully compiled figures of Mr. Seward,[1] we find that there was, according to the census of 1870, a Chinese population of 62,736, as against 34,933 in 1860. The following table, compiled by Mr. Alfred Wheeler, a witness before the Congressional Commission, is given by Mr. Seward.

YEAR.	ARRIVALS.	DEPARTURES.	GAIN.
1870	10,869	4,232	6,637
1871	5,542	3,264	2,278
1872	9,773	4,887	4,886
1873	17,075	6,805	10,270
1874	16,085	7,710	8,375
1875	18,021	6,305	11,716
1876 to Oct. 1st.	13,914	3,481	10,433
	91,279	36,684	54,595

The Chinese population at the end of 1876 would have been, then, 62,736, plus 54,595, or 117,331; a deduction of two per cent. for the natural death-rate leaves 104,731.

---

[1] Chinese Immigration in its Social and Economical Aspects. N. Y., 1881.

The Alta (California) newspaper carries the figures
on from 1876, as follows.

YEAR.	ARRIVALS.	DEPARTURES.	GAIN.	LOSS.
1877	9,906	7,852	2,054	—
1878	7,418	6,512	906	—
1879	6,544	6,906	—·—	362
	23,868	21,270	2,960	362
Gain				2,598
Estimated death-rate				6,000
Falling off in Chinese population . . .				3,402

From a· study of these figures, which are fairly
well verified by the results of our census of 1880,
which gives us a Chinese population of 105,448, Mr.
Seward concludes that the number of Chinese in this
country has remained nearly stationary since 1876.

We can thus see that we cannot account for the
increase in smoking-opium imported on the score of
an increase in our Chinese population.

As the smoking of opium by Americans was beginning to spread with greatest rapidity at the beginning of 1877, let us see how the increase in imports of smoking-opium is tabled :

In 1876, 53,189.42 lbs.
" 1877, 47,427.94 "   Falling off of 5,761.48 lbs.
" 1878, 54,804.78 "   Increase of   7,376.84 ⎫
" 1879, 60,647.67 "   "   "   5,842.89 ⎬ 29,768.06 lbs.
" 1880, 77,196.00 "   "   " 16,548.33 ⎭

Rather startling figures, and quite in keeping with the estimated spread of the vice amongst Americans. For, taking 100 grains a day as a fair average for an American smoker, multiply this by the 6,000 smokers, and the result by the number of days in a year, and we shall have, as the amount consumed by the American smokers to-day, 28,164 pounds.

A Chinese habitué smokes less daily than an American ; say about 60 grains. As about 20 per cent. of the Chinese smoke, we may say that there are 20,000 smoking. Multiply this by the number of days in the year, and the result by the daily quantity smoked, and we have 57,031 pounds consumed by the Chinamen.

	POUNDS
Consumed by American smokers	28,164
Chinese "	57,031
	85,195
Amount imported in 1880	77,196
	7,999

This would be an excess of 7,999 pounds smoked over and above that imported. This is readily accounted for by the amount smuggled, and the fact that many Chinamen cannot afford to smoke the best, or " No. 1 " opium, and use a mixture of gum opium—the ash left after smoking No. 1,

and No. 1 itself boiled together. The keepers of
some of the lowest dens do not use imported
opium at all, but make their own opium from the
gum.   It is said to be very powerful and very
rank.

The fact that a regular smoker will use 100
grains of opium each day would seem more surprising, did we not know that at least 33 per
cent. of it becomes ash, that it is still rich in morphia, six grains of it, hypodermically used, suffi-
cing to paralyze a rabbit.   Moreover, this ash, when
mixed with No. 1, and sold to the poorer smokers,
both here and in China, produces very decided
narcotic effects and serious physical ills that do
not obtain after the use of No. 1.   The ash, when
eaten, also produces a very decided effect.

CHAPTER II.

The early history of opium—Growth in India—Manner of raising and collecting the juice—Method of making "smoking-opium" in China.

THE medicinal properties of the juice of the poppy were well known as early as the third century before Christ, Theophrastus having referred to it under the name μηκώνιον. Next, in point of time, came Scribonius Largus, who, in his *Compositiones Medicamentorum*[1] (A.D. 40), pointed out the fact that the drug is derived, not from the foliage of the plant, but from the unripe capsules. In 77 Dioscorides[2] distinguished the juice of the capsule by the name ὀπός, from an extract of the whole plant μηκώνειον, which he considered much less active. He furthermore directed how and when the capsules should be incised in order to obtain the juice. Pliny and Celsus both speak of it. From this time on it is mentioned by numerous writers and travellers in different countries.

As the practice of opium-smoking is said by some

[1] (Ed. Bernhold, Argent, 1786, c. iii, sect. 22.) Quoted by Flückiger and Hanbury, London, 1879. I am deeply indebted to Flückiger and Hanbury, for many of the facts here given.

[2] Lib. iv, c. 55.

to have come to China from Egypt, it is interesting
to know that Unger [1] failed, in his investigations, to
trace any acquaintance of ancient Egypt with opium.

That the practice came to China from Arabia, as
is claimed by others, is completely negatived by the
fact that the religion of these people forbids the use
of any thing that has been burned or scorched
by fire.[2]   Hence, even the smoking of tobacco is
looked upon as a sin, and many stories are current
amongst the masses, where terrible punishment followed close upon indulgence in the weed.   There is
no doubt concerning the fact that the Arabians were,
at a very early date, well acquainted with medical
uses of opium, but that they ever smoked it, is, I
think, definitely negatived by the religious belief
above given.   Indeed, the Chinese derived the name
by which the drug is most commonly known, from
the Arabic, it being *o-fu-yung*, from *ufiyoon*.   Two
other names, *yapien* and *o-pien*, are adaptations of
the Chinese idiom to our word *opium*, which comes
from the Greek ὀπός (juice), as also does the Arabic
word *ufiyoon*.   There are several other Chinese terms
by which opium is called, and being translated are,
foreign poison, smoking dirt, black commodity, etc., etc.
In Hindu the drug is known as *ufeem*.   *Theriaka*,
consisting of opium, ambergris, saffron, and other
aromatics, was used as presents to kings and great

---

[1] Quoted by Flückiger and Hanbury. *Op. cit.*
[2] Palgrave: Central and Eastern Arabia, London, 1873, pp. 212, 282.

men. Another confection, *el mogen* (magoon or
madgoon), is to be found at Cairo, and consists of
opium and hyoscyamus. In Borneo, opium and tobacco are smoked together.[1]

The introduction of opium into India, from which
China gets her chief supply, is thought by Flückiger
and Hanbury to have been connected with the spread
of Islamism, and may have been favored by the
Mohammedan prohibition of wine. The earliest
mention of it in that country is made by Barbosa,[2]
who visited Calicut, on the Malabar coast, in 1511.

Opium is obtained from the capsules of the white
poppy or *papaver somniferum.* That which reaches
China, as has already been said, comes chiefly from
India, the whole trade being in the hands of the
East India Company.

" The principal region of British India distinguished for the production of opium, is the central
tract of the Ganges, comprising an area of about 600
miles in length by 200 miles in width. It reaches
from Dinajpur in the east to Hazaribagh in the
south and Gorakhpur in the north, and extends
westward to Agra, thus including the flat and
thickly populated districts of Behar and Benares.
The amount of land here actually under poppy cultivation, was estimated in 1871–72 as 560,000 acres.
The region second in importance for the culture of

---

[1] Calkins: Opium and the Opium Habit, Phila., 1871.
[2] Coasts of East Africa and Malabar, London, 1866.

opium, consists of the broad table-lands of Malwa
and the slopes of the Vindhya Hills, in the domin-
ion of the Holkar."[1]   The poppy is raised in other
parts of India, but in nothing like the quantity furnished by the above-named districts.

The greater part of the poppy cultivation in India
is a government monopoly, small enterprises being
here and there carried on by private individuals and
companies.

The mode of raising the poppy in the Patna district is as follows:

" The ryot, or cultivator, having selected a piece of ground,
always preferring (*cæteris paribus*) that which is nearest his house,
fences it in.   He then, by repeated ploughings, makes it completely
fine, and removes all the weeds and grass.   Next, he divides the field
into two or more beds by small dykes of mold, running lengthwise or
crosswise, according to the slope and nature of the ground, and again
into smaller squares by dykes leading from the principal ones.   A
tank, about ten feet deep, is dug at one end of the field, from which,
by means of a leathern bucket, water is raised into one of the principal dykes and carried to every part as required.   This irrigation is
necessary, because the cultivation is carried on in dry weather.   The
seed is sown in November and the juice collected in February and
March, during a period, usually, of about six weeks.   Weeding and
watering commence as soon as the plants spring up, and are continued
until the poppies come to maturity."

" Cuts are then made with a small shell or knife in the rind of the
seed-vessels ; from them the juice exudes during the night and is
scraped off in the morning.   When the heads are exhausted they
become whitish."[2]

[1] Flückiger and Hanbury, *op. cit.*, p. 50.
[2] Chinese Repository, vol. v, p. 472, Williams, *op. cit.*

This process of obtaining the juice (known by Galen as *lachryma papaveris*, or poppy tears) was accurately described by Dioscorides more than 1800 years ago.

Opium from different countries (Asia-Minor, Persia, India, China, Egypt, England, Australia, America, Scotland, and Algeria), and from different parts of the same country, varies much in the proportion of its ingredients, due in part to adulteration and in part to soil peculiarity and atmospheric influences. Thus French opium is noted for its richness in morphine (14.50 –22.80 per cent.), as also is that of Asia-Minor (14.78 per cent.), America (Vermont), (15.75 per cent.), and Persia (10.8 –13.47 per cent.); that of Egypt less so (5.8 per cent.) East India opium stands the lowest in the scale as regards the percentage of morphine (2.48 –3.21 per cent.).[1] This makes little difference, however, to the Chinese, who select their opium, not for its strength, but for its flavor, etc. India opium is noticeable for containing a large proportion of *narcotine* (7.7 per cent). Opium grown in China contains a somewhat larger per cent. of morphine (5.9 per cent.) than is found in India opium, and about the same amount of narcotine (7.5 per cent.). The natives, however, prefer the imported drug, which is brought to them by the ton. The poppy is now grown in the Yunnan,

---

[1] Flückiger and Hanbury, *op. cit.*

Szechuen, and Kweichow provinces, the annual
yield of opium being about 41,000 peculs, or 5,466,-
666 pounds.[1]

In the year ending March 31, 1872, about 12,000,-
000 pounds of opium reached China from British
India.[2]

Flückiger and Hanbury describe the manner of
incising the capsule and gathering the juice a little
differently from the account in the Chinese Repos-
tory:

In Behar the sowing takes place at the beginning of November,
and the capsules are scarified in February or March (March or April
in Malwa). This operation is performed with a peculiar instrument
called a *nutshur*, having three or four two-pointed blades bound
together with cotton thread. In using the *nutshur* only one set of
points is brought into use at a time, the capsule being scarified verti-
cally from base to summit. This scarification is repeated on different
sides of the capsule, at intervals of a few days, from two to six
times. In many districts of Bengal transverse cuts are made in the
poppy-head, as in Asia Minor.

The milky juice is scraped on early in the following morning
with an iron scoop, which, as it becomes filled, is emptied into an
earthen pot carried by the collector's side. In Malwa a flat scraper
is used, which, as well as the fingers of the gatherer, is wetted from
time to time in linseed oil, to prevent the adhesion of the glutinous
juice. All accounts represent the juice as being in a very moist state
by reason of the dew, which even sometimes washes it away.

The juice, when brought home, is a wet, granular mass of pinkish

---

[1] Recent reports state that the poppy is now cultivated to some extent in
thirteen provinces of China.

[2] (Annual Statement of the Trade and Navigation of British India with
Foreign Countries, published by order of the Governor-General, Culcutta,
1872, p. 52.) Flückiger and Hanbury, *op. cit.*, p. 53.

color, and in the bottom of the vessel in which it is contained there collects a dark fluid resembling coffee, which is called *pasēwā*. The recent juice strongly reddens litmus and blackens metallic iron. It is placed in a shallow earthen vessel, which is tilted in such a manner that the *pasēwā* may drain off as long as there is any of it to be separated. This liquor is set aside in a covered vessel. The residual mass is now exposed to the air, though never to the sun, and turned over every few days to promote its attaining the proper degree of dryness, which, according to the Benares regulations, allows of 30 per cent. of moisture. This drying operation occupies three or four wee

The drug is then taken to the government factory for sale ; previous to being sold it is examined for adulteration by a native expert, and its proportion of water is also carefully determined. Having been received into stock it under goes but little treatment, beyond a thorough mixing, until it is required to be formed into globular cakes. First, the quantity of opium is weighed out, and having been formed into a ball, is enveloped in a crust of dried poppy petals, skilfully agglutinated one over the other by means of a liquid called *lewa*. This consists partly of good opium, partly of *pasēwā*, and partly of opium of inferior quality, all being mixed with the washings of the various pots and vessels which have contained opium, and then evaporated to a thick fluid, 100 gr. of which should afford 53 of dry residue.

The finished balls, usually called *cakes*, which are quite spherical and have a diameter of six inches, are rolled in poppy-trash, which is the name given to the coarsely powdered stalks, capsules, and leaves of the plant. They are then placed in small dishes and exposed directly to the rays of the sun. Should any become distended it is at once opened, the gas allowed to escape, and the cake made up again. After three days the cakes are placed (by the end of July) in frames in the factory, where the air is allowed to circulate. They still, however, require constant watching and turning, as they are liable to contract mildew, which has to be removed by rubbing in *poppy-trash*. By October the cakes have become perfectly dry externally and quite hard, and are in condition to be packed in cases (40 cakes in each) for the Chinese market, which consumes the great bulk of the manufacture.

The first venture of the East India Company to carry opium to China was in 1773, the Portugese having opened the trade in 1767. In a short time the business spread with tremendous rapidity, flooding China with opium, and enriching the merchants engaged in the speculation. In 1820 the Chinese government, recognizing the terrible ascendancy the vice of opium-smoking was obtaining over its subjects, and feeling the great drain in money that was leaving the country annually to pay for the drug, an edict was issued by the emperor [1] against the traffic in any form, and forbidding any vessel having opium on board to enter port.

This was almost wholly disregarded both by the native merchants and by the English. Smuggling by means of bribing the too willing officials, was carried on openly.

Finally, matters came to such a pass that the English merchants and residents were imprisoned and held until all opium, on land and in ships, was surrendered to the authorities; 20,283 chests, valued at eleven million dollars, were seized and destroyed. It being found impossible to settle matters amicably, the British government, claiming that their

---

[1] Shuck: Portfolio Chinensis, Macao, China, 1840.

subjects had been unjustly imprisoned and their property destroyed, declared war against China, who was simply endeavoring to protect her subjects from an overwhelming vice, and carried the country at the point of the bayonet. This futile effort of a so-called heathen emperor to shield his people from a vice that threatened physical, mental, and moral destruction, and the successful endeavor of a Christian nation, on a flimsy pretext of insult to its subjects, to force upon them the vice so thoroughly dreaded, makes a picture that must have engendered sorrow in heaven and mirthful satisfaction in hell. By means of a second war, in 1860, the English compelled the Chinese government to legalize the traffic.

The Chinese method of preparing opium for smoking is very fully described by Williams,[1] as follows.

The utensils used for preparing opium for smoking consists chiefly of three hemispherical brass pans, two bamboo filters, two portable furnaces, earthen pots, ladles, straining cloths, and sprinklers. The ball[2] being cut in two, the interior is taken out and the opium adhering to, or contained in the leafy covering is previously simmered three several times, each time using a pint of spring water, and straining it into an earthen pot ; some cold water is poured over the dregs after the third boiling, and from half a cake (weighing at

---

[1] The Middle Kingdom, a Survey of the Geography, Government, Education, Social Life, Arts, Religion, etc., of the Chinese Empire. New York, 1879.

[2] In India, the juice of the poppy, dried to about 70 per cent. spissitude, is rolled in balls and packed in strong boxes, the weight being from 116 to 140 lbs., according to the variety ; that from the Malwa weighing more than that from the Patna district   There are 40 balls rolled in dried poppy leaves in each chest.

first about 28 lbs., and with which this process is supposed to be conducted) there will be about five pints of liquid. The interior of the cake is then boiled with this liquid for about an hour, until all is reduced to a paste, which is spread out with a spatula in two pans and exposed to the fire for two or three minutes at a time, till the water is all driven off ; during this operation it is often broken up and respread, and at the last drying, cut across with a knife. It is all then spread out in one cake and covered with six pints of water, and allowed to remain several hours or over night for digestion. When sufficiently soaked, a rag filter is placed on the edge of the pan and the whole of the valuable part drips slowly through the rag into a basket lined with coarse bamboo paper, from which it falls into the other brass pan, about as much liquid going through as there was water poured over the cake. The dregs are again soaked and immediately filtered till found to be nearly tasteless. This weaker part usually makes about six pints of liquid.

The first six pints are then briskly boiled, being sprinkled with cold water to allay the heat so as not to boil over, and removing the scum with a feather into a separate vessel. After boiling twenty minutes, five pints of the weak liquid are poured in and boiled with it, until the whole is evaporated to about three pints, when it is strained through paper into another pan, and the remaining pint thrown into the pan just emptied, to wash away any portion that may remain in it, and also boiled a little while, when it is also strained into the three pints.

The whole is then placed over a slow fire in the small furnace and boiled down to a proper consistency for smoking. While it is evaporating, a ring forms around the edge, and the pan is taken off the fire at intervals to prolong the process, the mass being, the while, rapidly stirred with sticks, and fanned, until it becomes thick like treacle, when it is taken out and put into small pots for smoking.

The dregs, containing the vegetable residuum, together with the scum and washings of the pans, are lastly strained and boiled with water, producing about six pints of thin, brownish liquid, which is evaporated to a proper consistence for selling to the poor.

The process of seething the crude opium is exceedingly unpleasant to those unaccustomed to it, from the overpowering narcotic fumes which arise; and this odor marks every shop where it is prepared, and every person who smokes it. The loss of weight by this mode of preparation is about one half. The Malays prepare it in much the same manner. The custom in Penang is to reduce the dry cake, made on the first evaporation, to a powder; and when it is digested and again strained and evaporated, reducing it to a consistence resembling shoemaker's wax.

There are two grades of No. 1 smoking-opium that come to us, the Li Yun and the Fuk Lung, varying in price from $7.75 to $8.20 a can. The duty on this is $6.00 per pound. Smoking-opium prepared in this country is called Bach Yun, as against Kung Yun, which means the Chinese preparation irrespective of grade.

CHAPTER III.

Description of the "lay-out," pipe, etc., etc.—Manner of smoking
—English, American, and Chinese smoking-places.

SO much misconception exists, and so many
false statements have been made as to how
opium is smoked, and with what kind of a pipe,
that I feel it my duty to describe in detail the
method and the apparatus.

For instance, a writer in *Blackwood's Magazine*,[1]
otherwise accurate, makes the following curiously
false statement :

"The Chinese extract from Indian opium all that
water will dissolve, generally from ½ to ¾ of its
weight, dry the dissolved extract and make it into
pills of the size of a pea ; one of these pills they put
into *a short, tiny pipe, often made of silver*,[2] inhale a
few puffs at a time, or one single, long puff, and return the smoke through the nostrils and *ears*[2] until
the necessary dose has been taken."

The same writer states, at another place, that
adepts in the practice blow the smoke out through
the *eyes, ears*, and nose.

---

[1] The Narcotics we Indulge in, *Blackwood*, Nov., 1853.

[2] Italics mine.

The opium-pipe, the origin and antiquity of which is wholly unknown, is the only one in which opium is or ever has been smoked.

It consists of two parts, a stem and a bowl. The stem is usually of bamboo, occasionally of orange-wood or sugar-cane, the former being so cut that it includes the space between two joints and about one quarter of the next space. The usual measurement is 24 inches in length, and four inches in circumference. Stems from 16 to 20 inches in length, and from 2 to 3 inches in circumference are imperfect, the bamboo being cut when too young or inferior pieces used. They do not color well and are not so easy to handle as the larger ones. New stems are of a straw color, but with long smoking become black and glossy. This is sometimes imitated by soaking the stem in dye-stuff.

A stem that has been long smoked becomes thoroughly satu-

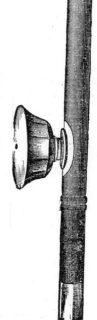

FIG. 1.—The Chinese Opium-Pipe.

rated with opium, which gives it a peculiar flavor much admired by old smokers. It is for this reason that the expensive and handsome ivory and porcelain stems sometimes seen, are not so highly valued, as they never "sweeten" with long usage.

The "lemon pipe" is one in which the stem, and sometimes the bowl, is made of rings of lemon peel, cemented together, layer over layer. When thoroughly dry, they are smoothed off and polished. They give a pleasant lemon odor to the smoke passing through them.

The Chinese, in preparing the better class of stems, "load" them with smoking-opium, previously "cooked," in order to give them a rich flavor.

At the junction of the middle with the lower third, or just back of the joint, a place is hollowed out of the side of the stem, and communicates with its longitudinal perforation.

About this hollow fits closely a shield of metal, usually brass, that rises in a rim above the hole. Into this is fitted the bowl. The stems may be plain, carved or ornamented with bands of silver, gold, or ivory. Good pipes usually have a button of ivory fitted on to, or screwed into the upper end of the stem, against which the lips are pressed during the smoking. The end of the stem, from the joint on, is partly for ornament, partly to equalize weight, and partly to render more convenient for holding.

The hollow space is used to hold papers or bits of rag.

The bowl, which is usually of a hard red clay, and hollow, may be bell-shaped, ovate, or hexagonal. On its under surface is a flange, or neck, by which it is fitted into the stem. This flange is usually chipped off, and its place taken by a metal rim which is fastened to the pipe-bowl by means of burnt alum. In order to make it fit tightly, this flange is ordinarily wrapped with a narrow piece of soft cloth. This is held in place by means of a little smoking-opium which, when dry, forms an excellent glue. The upper surface of the bowl is either flat or sloping slightly downward and outward. In its centre is an opening of about sufficient size to admit an ordinary darning-needle. The whole pipe is called the *Yen Tsiang*, or opium pistol.

The other articles necessary for a smoker's outfit are a box of buffalo-horn to contain the opium (*hop-toy*), a needle (*yen hauck*) on the end of which the opium is taken up, "cooked," and placed over the small opening in the upper surface of the bowl, a small glass lamp with a glass cover, perforated just above the flame, and in which sweet or peanut oil is burned, a pair of scissors for trimming the wick, (*kow ten*), a straight and curved knife for cleaning the bowl of the ash (*yen tshi*) that rapidly collects and renders the pipe foul, a saucer to hold this ash, a sponge with which, when wet, to cleanse and cool the upper surface of the bowl, and lastly, a tray upon which all these things rest.

The real Chinese tray consists of two parts, a small tray resting in the centre of a larger one. In

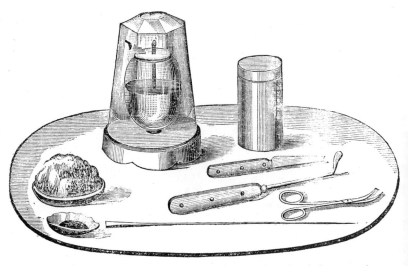

FIG. 2.—Smoker's Outfit: lamp, sponge, shell with opium, bowl-cleaners, scissors, needle, horn box for opium, and tray.

the small tray sit the lamp, two or more small boxes for opium, a receptacle for scissors and a place for the sponge. This tray is 12 inches long by 9 inches wide.

In the large tray rests the smaller one, a perfor-

ated rest for pipe bowls not in use, and three recep-
tacles, one for cigars and cigarettes, one for the ashes
from same, and the other for the *yen tshi*, or ashes
from the opium. This tray is 28 inches in length
by 18 inches in breadth. It has a flanged edge. It
may be of plain japanned ware or walnut or mahog-
any beautifully inlaid, and of variegated colors.
Some of those used by the wealthy Chinese are very
handsome.

The lamps, which are said to be made in Birming-
ham, England, are so constructed that the air entering at the base and emerging at the round hole at
the top keeps the flame steady and uniform.

The ordinary smoking-den, or " joint," is kept by
a Chinaman who speaks a little broken or " pigeon "
English. A segar-store, laundry, or small shop is
usually in front. Entering here, we pass into a rear
room fitted up for smoking. This is small, low-
ceilinged, dimly lighted, and uncarpeted. Around
three sides of the apartment runs a huge board shelf,
about four feet in width and two feet from the floor.
This is known as the bunk. Above this may run
another shelf of equal width, there being space
enough between the two to admit of a person sitting upright on the lower without his head touching
the upper shelf or platform, In the better class of
joints the platform is covered with matting, in some
by nothing. At an elevation of from six to eight

inches from the shelf, along the wall, there is a narrow board, sometimes plain, sometimes bevelled,
which serves as a head-rest for the smoker.   In
some places small narrow stools having the surface

Private Smoking Room in China, showing style of bunk, etc. It represents
a wealthy young man just commencing a downward career: he being in the
company of prostitutes.

padded are used as pillows instead of the narrow
strip of board.

In China there are vile dens for the poor, as well
as sumptuous apartments for the rich.   The former
are known as *Yin Kwan*, while the place for the

manufacture or preparation of the drug is called the
Yaon Kow.[1]

" The opium-shops in the cities (where the *hoi polloi*, the " filth and
scum," are prone to hive) are narrow rooms secluded from outside observation, dingy and dank, with a solitary lamp suspended midway,
apparently for the purpose of making darkness visible rather, and
which are packed almost to suffocation.   These dens of dissolute-
ness and debasement are but rarely visited by merchants and others
of the better class, unless with a view to greater privacy for the
time.[2]

"At the mansions of the rich there is usually found fitted up for the
accommodation of friends a private boudoir, richly ceiled, and gar-
nished with superb adornments, such as art only can achieve and
wealth procure ; and here rich paintings, with choice scraps from
Confucius, adorn the walls, and carvings in ivory, with other articles
of vertu, grace the tables.   Here, also, is provided in chief the gilded
opium-pipe, with all its appurtenances ; and here host and guest, un-
restrained by curious eyes, deliver themselves up without concern to
the inebriating chaudoo and its beatific transports." [3]

In London, in Ratcliffe Highway, just back of the
docks, there was a low den kept by one Lamar.   No
white men were smoking there.   Calkins speaks of
another place.[4]   He says :

" In the New Court, London, the camp-ground of a colony of foreigners, Chinese, Bengalese, Greeks, and others, is one of these
opium dens, under the direction of Ya-Hi, a man eighty years old and

---

[1] Portfolio Chinensis; being a collection of Chinese state papers, Shuck,
Macao, China. 1840, p. 177, note 19.
[2] Calkins : Opium and the Opium Appetite, Phila., 1871, p. 53.
[3] Huc : Travels Through China, N. Y., 1855.
[4] *Op. cit.*, p, 63.

himself an inveterate smoker, who makes the ordering of the nightly entertainment. Here in a close room, styled " the *Divan*," the air of which is enough to stifle a stranger, may be seen numerous visitors arranged squat around the tea-trays upon which their pipe-bowls rest, now indulging in vapid twaddle, now relapsing into idiotic mutterings, with the accompaniment of a motion of the lower jaw, sheep-fashion, or all may be quiet for the time, ready to break into mirthful extravagance at any instant, and for any or no cause. These people confess their willingness to work all day for procuring the furtive but fugitive enjoyment this receptacle holds out for the night."

Dickens, that master-hand at description, opens "The Mystery of Edwin Drood" in a low, squalid room in London, presided over by an old hag, and devoted to opium-smoking. He errs greatly, however, in his description of the manner of smoking and the effects obtained. The manufacture of a pipe-bowl out of a penny ink-bottle is truthful, for in the West, when short of bowls, this has been repeatedly done.

In *Scribner's Monthly* for July, 1880, George Francis Lathrop, under the very incorrect heading of " The Sorcery of Madjoon," attempts to describe some of the Chinese dens in this city. As the *Madjoon*, so called, or more properly *El Mogen*, is the name of a conserve that is eaten and not smoked by the inhabitants of Cairo, its use in this connection is entirely wrong. The cut that accompanies the article is as incorrect as the article itself, the devotee being represented as sitting up and smoking the *yen tsiang* as an ordinary person would a tobacco-pipe. It is to these carelessly written and highly colored descriptions that the mistaken ideas held by the masses generally may be ascribed.

A smoker entering one of the dens or "joints" in this city, removes his shoes, coat, and collar, hangs them upon a peg, and stretching himself transversely across the platform beside a tray containing the apparatus, calls for a pipe and some opium. The usual call is for "two bits'" or twenty-five cents' worth. For this money the Chinaman gives from 6 to 10 "fān" (35 to 60 gr.) of No. 1 or first-class, and from 12 to 20 "fān" (70 to 120 gr.) of No. 2 or second-class opium.

Having the necessary article and materials, the smoker settles himself comfortably upon his side, takes up a little of the treacle-like mass of opium upon the steel needle, or *yen hauck*, and holding it above the flame of the lamp, watches it bubble and swell to six or seven times its original size. In doing so it loses its inky hue, and becomes of a bright golden-brown color, and gives off a pleasant creamy odor much admired by old smokers. Poor opium does not yield so pleasant an odor, is liable to drop from the needle into the lamp, and rarely gives so handsome a color, the yellow being, here and there, streaked with black. This process is known as "cooking" the opium. Having brought it to a

proper consistence, the operator, with a rapid twirl-
ing motion of the fingers, rolls the mass upon the
smooth surface of the bowl, submitting it occasionally to the flame, now and then catching it upon the
edge and drawing it out into strings in order to cook
it through more thoroughly. This is called *chying*[1]
the mass. Rolling it again upon the surface of the
bowl until the opium is formed into a small pea-
sized mass, with the needle as a centre, the needle
is forced down into the small hole in the bowl,
thus levelling off the bottom of the pea.[2] Then
grasping the stem of the pipe, near the bowl, in the
left hand, the bowl is held across the flame of the
lamp to warm it a little, the bottom of the opium
mass is warmed, and by again thrusting the needle
into the small aperture in the centre of the bowl
and quickly withdrawing it, the mass, with a hole in
its centre, is left upon the surface of the bowl, it
surrounding the hole that communicates with that
of the stem. Inclining the body slightly forward,
the smoker tips the pipe-bowl across the lamp until
the flame strikes the opium. Inhaling strongly and
steadily, the smoke of the burning drug passes into
the lungs of the operator and is returned through
the nose. This smoke is heavy, white, and has a not
unpleasant fruity odor. It is hardly necessary to say

---

[1] The Chinese words here, as elsewhere, are spelled as near the sound as
possible, and may in some instances be incorrect, so far, at least, as the spelling
is concerned.

[2] Known as the chaudoo (tschaudu).

that the smoke never passes out through the ears
and eyes.   Having finished this bolus which re-
quires but one long or a few short inspirations, the
smoker cools the bowl of the pipe with a sponge
and repeats the operation as often as is necessary
to obtain the desired effect.   Smokers are classed
as " long-draw " and " short-draw " men, according
as they consume the pill in one or several inhalations.   The long draw is undoubtedly the most injurious.

The wealthier smokers, here and in the East, do
not visit these joints, but have rooms fitted up in
Oriental style, where a few friends meet to enjoy the
pleasures of the pipe.   Unlike other forms of the
opium-habit, that by smoking finds a special inducement in companionship, especially if the companions
are congenial.   Men and women often meet to
smoke, talk, and enjoy that state that comes as near
as it is possible for an American to come to the
dolce far niente of the Italian.   In the joints, two
persons, sometimes three, are usually found about
the one tray, one cooking while the other smokes,
and *vice versa*.   A package of cigarettes will usually be found upon the tray, they being smoked
" between pipes."

To be able to "cook" well is quite an art, and one
of which an old smoker is very proud.   A novice or
a poor cook will bedaub himself and the pipe, and

either overdo or underdo the opium, so that it is too sticky or too crisp to smoke well.

A man who smokes large amounts of opium daily is, in this country, called a " fiend." Some Americans have a curious nomenclature for smokers, based upon the number of times in the day and the hour at which a person smokes. Thus, a man who smokes three times is said to have a " triple habit," one who smokes but once, the " single habit, "one who smokes early, "the early habit," etc., etc. This is manifestly incorrect.

As to a mixture of habits, I find that it is a rare thing for a smoker to be at the same time an opium- or morphine-taker, save in this way : when on long journeys, or in places where a pipe cannot be had, he will usually cook up a number of pellets of smoking-opium, and take enough of these by the mouth to carry him without discomfort beyond his time for smoking. Occasionally we meet with smokers who are at the same time using opium or morphine by the mouth. This is, however, very rare. I have had one such patient under treatment. Some smokers are of the firm belief that should they swallow a little of the smoking-opium in its raw state certain death would result. This is of course nonsensical. I have taken as high as six grains myself without any ill effects whatever. Many have the idea, evidently taken from the Chinese, that should the *yen hauck* be thrust through a roach or bed-bug just before taking up the opium upon it, a most horrible and agonizing death will certainly visit the one who smokes that pellet.

Women are never allowed to smoke a good pipe, the Chinese entertaining the belief that it would result in splitting of the stem and a failure to color. There is some truth in this, for moisture will often split the bamboo stems, and it is a notable fact that when women smoke, saliva will, as a rule, get into the aperture against which the lips are placed.

CHAPTER IV.

Immediate effects upon the novice—Fallacies regarding dreams, sleep, etc.—Danger of smoking after hard drinking —Symptoms of abstinence—A smoker's letter.

AS vague and incorrect ideas of the immediate and remote effects produced by opium-smoking are held by people generally as there are regarding the kind of pipe used and the manner of smoking. Thus Dickens, in his "Mystery of Edwin Drood," gives us the following :

THE DAWN.

An ancient English Cathedral Tower ! How can the ancient English Cathedral Tower be here ! The well-known massive gray square tower of its old Cathedral ? How can that be here ! There is no spike of rusty iron in the air, between the eye and it, from any point of the real prospect. What is the spike that intervenes, and who has set it up ? Maybe it is set up by the Sultan's orders for the impaling of a horde of Turkish robbers, one by one. It is so, for cymbals clash, and the Sultan goes by to his palace in long procession. Ten thousand cimeters flash in the sunlight, and thrice ten thousand dancing-girls strew flowers. Then follow white elephants, caparisoned in countless gorgeous colors, and infinite in number and attendants. Still the Cathedral Tower rises in the background, where it cannot be, and still no writhing figure is on the grim spike. Stay ! Is the spike so low a thing as the rusty spike on the top of a post of an old bedstead that has tumbled all awry ?   Some vague period of drowsy laughter must be devoted to the consideration of this possibility.

Shaking from head to foot, the man whose scattered consciousness has thus fantastically pieced itself together at length rises, supports his trembling frame upon his arms, and looks around.   He is in the meanest and closest of small rooms.   Through the ragged window-curtain, the light of early day steals in from a miserable court.   He lies, dressed, across a large unseemly bed, upon a bedstead that has indeed given way under the weight upon it.   Lying, also dressed and also across the bed, not long-wise, are a Chinaman, a Lascar, and a haggard woman.   The first two are in a sleep or stupor ; the last is blowing at a kind of pipe, to kindle it.   And as she blows, and, shading it with her lean hand, concentrates its red spark of light, it serves in the dim morning as a lamp to show him what he sees of her.

" Another ? " says this woman in a querulous, rattling whisper. " Have another ? "

He looks about him, with his hand to his forehead.

" Ye 've smoked as many as five since ye come in at midnight," the woman goes on, as she chronically complains.   " Poor me, poor me, my head is so bad !   Them two come in after ye.   Ah, poor me, the business is slack, is slack !   Few Chinamen about the docks, and fewer Lascars, and no ships coming in, these say !   Here's another ready for ye, deary.   Ye 'll remember, like a good soul, won't ye, that the market price is dreffle high just now ?   More nor three shillings and sixpence for a thimbleful !   And ye 'll remember that nobody but me (and Jack Chinaman t' other side the court ; but he can't do it as well as me) has the true secret of mixing it ?   Ye 'll pay up according, deary, won't ye ? "

She blows at the pipe as she speaks, and occasionally bubbling at it, inhales much of its contents.

" O me, O me, my lungs is weak, my lungs is bad !   It 's nearly ready for ye, deary.   Ah, poor me, poor me, my poor hand shakes like to drop off !   I see ye coming-to, and I ses to my poor self, ' I 'll have another ready for him, and he 'll bear in mind the market

price of opium, and pay according.' O my poor head ! I makes my
pipes of old penny ink-bottles, ye see, deary—this is one,—and I fits
in a mouthpiece, this way, and I takes my mixter out of this thimble
with this little horn-spoon, and so I fills, deary. Ah, my poor nerves!
I got Heavens-hard drunk for sixteen year afore I took to this ; but
this don't hurt me, not to speak of. And it takes away the hunger
as well as wittles, deary."

She hands him the nearly emptied pipe, and sinks back, turning
over on her face.

He rises unsteadily from the bed, lays the pipe upon the hearth-
stone, draws back the ragged curtain, and looks with repugnance at
his three companions. He notices that the woman has opium-smoked
herself into a strange likeness of the Chinaman. His form of cheek,
eye, and temple, and his color, are repeated in her.   Said Chinaman
convulsively wrestles with one of his many gods, or devils, perhaps,
and snarls horribly.   The Lascar laughs, and dribbles at the mouth.
The hostess is still.

" What visions can *she* have ? " the waking man muses, as he turns
her face toward him, and stands looking down at it.   " Visions of
many butchers' shops, and public-houses, and much credit ?   Of an
increase of hideous customers, and this horrible bedstead set upright
again, and this horrible court swept clean ?   What can she rise to,
under any quantity of opium, higher than that !—Eh ? "

He bends down his ear, to listen to her mutterings.

" Unintelligible ! "

As he watches the spasmodic shoots and darts that break out of her
face and limbs, like fitful lightning out of a dark sky, some conta-
gion in them seizes upon him, insomuch that he has to withdraw himself to a lean arm-chair by the hearth—placed there, perhaps, for
such emergencies—and to sit in it, holding tight, until he has got
the better of this unclean spirit of imitation.

Then he comes back, pounces on the Chinaman, and seizing him
with both hands by the throat, turns him violently on the bed.   The
Chinaman clutches the aggressive hands, resists, gasps, and protests.

" What do you say ? "

A watchful pause.

" Unintelligible ! "

Slowly loosening his grasp as he listens to the incoherent jargon with an attentive frown, he turns to the Lascar and fairly drags him forth upon the floor. As he falls, the Lascar starts into a half-risen attitude, glares with his eyes, lashes about him fiercely with his arms, and draws a phantom knife. It then becomes apparent that the woman has taken possession of his knife, for safety's sake ; for, she too, starting up, and restraining and expostulating with him, the knife is visible in her dress, not in his, when they drowsily drop back, side by side.

There has been chattering and clattering enough between them, but to no purpose. When any distinct word has been flung into the air, it has had no sense or sequence. Wherefore " unintelligible ! " is again the comment of the watcher, made with some reassured nodding of his head, and a gloomy smile. He then lays certain silver money on the table, finds his hat, gropes his way down the broken stairs, gives a good-morning to some rat-ridden doorkeeper, in bed in a black hutch beneath the stairs, and passes out.

That same afternoon, the massive gray square tower of an old Cathedal rises before the sight of a jaded traveller. The bells are going for daily vesper service, and he must needs attend it, one would say, from his haste to reach the open Cathedral door. The choir are getting on their sullied white robes, in a hurry, when he arrives among them, gets on his own robe, and falls into the procession filing in to service. Then the Sacristan locks the iron-barred gates that divide the sanctuary from the chancel, and all of the procession, having scuttled into their places, hide their faces ; and then the intoned words, " WHEN THE WICKED MAN—" rise among groins of arches and beams of roof, awakening muttered thunder.

The awakening from the opium sleep is wholly incorrect, for if an habitué does sleep after smoking (it being a rare thing to do so), he awakes suddenly and apparently with the full powers of his mind. The mistaking a nail in a bedpost for a spike on a cathedral-tower belongs more to the waking dream of the hashish-eater than to the opium-smoker, as also do the brilliant imagery of the procession and the dancing-girls.

Furthermore, if this man was an habitué, as we are led to believe from his familiarity with the place and its occupants, and from the old hag's conversation, five "pipes" of opium would have had but very little effect upon him,—would not certainly have sent him to sleep; nor would he have left the den after this number and gone to a place where it was doubtful if he could smoke soon again. A smoker expecting to be away from the pipe for a longer or shorter time, *always* smokes to decided excess, from fifty to one hundred pipes, and then carries himself along for succeeding days on pills of cooked opium. The old woman's effort to "kindle the pipe" is absurd, for no kindling is necessary, the whole process being conducted by the smoker himself over the lamp. The "mixing" is all done in China, unless adulteration is meant. The pipe is never "filled," except with ash; and a steel needle, and not a "horn-spoon," is the instrument employed.

There is a world of truth in the expression, "I got Heavens-hard drunk for sixteen years," etc., made by the old woman, for I know of several instances where hard drinkers, commencing to use the pipe, entirely abandoned alcoholics.

Commencing with the experience of a novice, let us follow the effects of opium-smoking through those produced upon an habitual and excessive smoker, or "fiend." Take my own case first. Knowing that I should be better able to judge of the effects if I smoked the drug myself, I tried the experiment a number of times, both at "a joint" and at home, where I had every facility, having purchased a full "lay-out" and had a Chinese bunk erected in my office.

The first effect was nausea, dizziness, accompanied by a pleasant sense of exhilaration, and followed by a quiet, easy contentment. This was after deeply inhaling four "pipes." There was an increase in the force and frequency of the pulse, hot flashes over the body and face. After a few more pipes came a soft pulse, lessened in frequency, a fall in temperature, giddiness, a slight nausea, with some staggering on rising or walking ; then profuse perspiration, ringing in the ears, intense itching of the nose, eyelids, face, scrotum, and back. Profuse perspiration and nausea continued, followed shortly by abundant but easy vomiting. There was also a feeling of uncertainty in putting down the feet in walking, dazing of the mind, sleepiness, heaviness of the eyelids, contraction of the pupils, dryness of the throat, and a fear to cross the street if a wagon or car was approaching. There seemed to be some trouble with the ears, for I found myself talking very loud. The sexual appetite was increased.

This was followed by intense sleepiness, the daze, however, lasting but a moment and the awakening being sudden. There were no dreams. The nausea, which was a prominent and distressing symptom in my case, lasted for the next twenty-four hours, as also did the itching. The following is typical of many experiments made on myself.

FIRST EXPERIMENT.

	PULSE.	TEMPERATURE.	RESPIRATION.	SPHYGMOGRAM.
Before smoking	80	98.5	22	
1st stage (Exhilaration)	110	98.8	22	Rise in tension; sharp, long up-stroke.
2d stage (Commencing nausea)	118	99.5	20	Blunting of end of up-stroke; tension stationary.
3d stage (Sleepiness, nausea, itching)	70–58	98	14	Up-stroke again high and sharp; hyper-dicrotism.

The pulse indicated nervousness and exhaustion for the following 24 hours. Tactile sensibility was decidedly increased during the same time. Urine pale, abundant; specific gravity 1,010 (1,020 at other times); reaction neutral and highly phosphatic; contained a trace of morphia.

The results in each experiment, with the exception of minor degrees of variation, were the same. Once, after smoking ten pipes, the pulse fell in the fourth hour to 41 and remained so for six hours.

In order to see whether an equivalent amount of morphia by the mouth would have the same effect, I took three quarters of a grain, which would be equal to the amount in the opium I had inhaled. The results obtained were as follows :

	PULSE.	TEMPERATURE.	RESPIRATION.	SPHYGMOGRAM.
Before taking	70	98.4	18	
For 1st hour	90	98.4	16	Increase in tension.
For 3d hour	98	98.5	17	" "
After 3 hours' sleep	90	98.2	16	As before taking.

There was slight nausea, no vomiting, some itching of the nose, no flashes of heat, no sweating, no ill effect the following day. The urine was found to be of an amber color; sp. gr. 1,018 ; acid, non-phosphatic, and containing morphia. Three quarters of a grain was really more than one would get in smoking 18 grains of opium, for I have found that all the morphia is not taken up in the process of preparing, and a considerable amount is to be found in the ash after smoking, six grains of the ash producing a condition of partial paralysis in a full-sized female rabbit when injected hypodermically. Furthermore, while the sleep following the smoking was calm and perfectly free from dreams, that following the taking of morphia was filled with horrible phantasmagoria.

Knowing that morphia always affects me unpleasantly, and fearing that I might not be a fair subject for these experiments, I repeated them upon one lady and two gentlemen just commencing to smoke habitually, with the same results.

The following is the experience of one of my male nurses, who kindly tried smoking to permit of my experimenting on him. I give it in his own words. He is a man who is perfectly honest and trustworthy, and one not given to exaggeration or an unbridled imagination. Furthermore, he was entirely ignorant of the effect of smoking to excess. The effect upon the pulse is the more conclusive from the fact that in his case, in health, the tension is very low, and the first down-stroke almost reaches the base line.

Fred'k K., æt. 35, M., weight 185 lbs., had taken opium before, by the mouth, without any ill effects.

"July 12, 1881, 2 P.M., I commenced smoking with an habitué, who "cooked" the opium, he and I consuming alternate pipes.[1] On smoking seven pipes I felt a little exhilarated, and continued to feel

---

[1] The word pipe as here used means the opium used at a single smoking.

so until an hour after smoking the ninth pipe. At this time the feeling of exhilaration increased. I felt very talkative, and wished to smoke more, but by Dr. Kane's advice stopped after the tenth pipe. At 6.30 P.M. there was itching of different parts of the body and some nausea. I became very pale. This feeling lasted about twenty minutes. Drank two cups of tea and ate a little supper. Felt natural until about 10 P.M., when nausea rapidly came on, and I suddenly vomited. There was no straining in the act. Read until about 12 midnight. Retired, and was on the point of sleeping when I was possessed with a sudden dread of doing so. Although very sleepy I felt that if I allowed myself to doze I should jump out of the window, and as I occupied a room on the third floor I was in great terror. I tried several times to reason myself out of the belief, but though I knew that I was extremely foolish to fear such a thing, I could not do so. Finally I was forced to get up and shut the blinds, fastening them securely, close the windows at the top and bottom, light the gas, and place chairs between the bed and the windows, so that if I attempted to reach the windows I would stumble, make a noise and wake myself. Again I tried to sleep, but when just dropping off I would start and look around the room, thinking there was something or somebody there. I would then try to calm myself, saying to myself how foolish and nervous I was. I thought that if I had a rope I could secure myself so as to prevent accidents. I went down on to the first floor, but could not find one. I then listened to see if any of the patients or their nurses were awake, so that I might pass the night with them. But I could not hear a sound. I returned to my room and again tried to sleep, but could in no way overcome my fear of jumping through the window. I lit the gas again, and read and pottered about until 4.30 A.M. On attempting to look out of the window I was obliged to pull my head in, as it seemed as if I must jump out. I then went out into the yard and walked about until people were stirring. At 8 A.M. I ate a hearty breakfast, and at 9 A.M. tried again to sleep. On the fourth attempt I succeeded. Slept till 12 M.; rose and ate a hearty lunch. During the night of the 12th and the succeeding day I seemed to smell the opium cooking and could taste it. My arms felt like lead. All that day I felt as I should imagine a person would feel after a week's drunk."

Normal pulse	68
After smoking three pipes	84
After ten pipes	84
The next day	108

During the smoking and for 24 hours afterward, the pupils were firmly contracted. I regret that I did not take the pulse during the night. This is of course not a fair example of the effects of moderate smoking on a novice, for Mr. K. certainly smoked to excess. The gentleman who was smoking with him was a " fiend," and made very " large pipes," that is to say, used about double the ordinary amount of opium each time. As each smoked the same amount, Mr. K. must have used 74 grains in the course of three hours. This is nearly equal to 150 grains of crude opium. One third of the 74 grains became ash. Smoking several times subsequently in smaller quantity produced no such effect. Another of my nurses, illustrating the variable susceptibilities of different persons to this drug, smoked nine large and three small pipes in the course of two hours without any effect save a slowing of the pulse. Subsequently, however, after trying the " long draw," the effect was very decided.

F. R. S., Am., 23, nurse, single, wt. 115 lbs.,

smoked eight pipes on afternoon of 25th inst. Had smoked nine pipes on afternoon of 23d, with no effect, on account of not inhaling smoke properly.

At the end of fourth pipe began to feel a drowsiness similar to a person partly under the influence of an anæsthetic. Slight dizziness upon attempting to stand, itching, etc. After smoking eighth pipe limbs felt heavy, head felt twice its natural size, increased drowsiness, itching, etc. Went to bed but couldn't sleep on account of itching in all parts of the body, which counterbalanced pleasant effects that old smokers speak of. Four hours after smoking entire left side felt as though under a heavy weight. Severe palpitation of heart (which only lasted ten minutes,) violent twitching of muscles of left eyelid, etc. Nine hours after smoking attempted to urinate but found it impossible. Succeeded two hours later, however. Pulse 40, which arose to 60, after taking $\frac{1}{48}$ gr. atropia.

Pupils greatly contracted.

Now, twenty hours after smoking, feels very languid; no appetite; headache, etc.

The symptoms which he has described are not the result of imagination, as they are the exact reverse of what he expected.

Smoking to excess, especially after hard drinking, is very dangerous. A young man, Mr. D., a very hard smoker now, was taken to a "joint" by a friend, one night, some two years ago. Both had been drinking hard for several days, and at the time of entering the place were still under the influence of liquor. Mr. D.'s friend was an habitué. Mr. D. had never smoked before. His friend quietly cooked and smoked, leaving Mr. D. to the care of two Chinamen who were cooking for him. After smoking for a long time, and a quantity of opium ($1.25 worth, 50 "fun," or about 325 grs.), Mr. D.'s head fell back, he suddenly became of a blackish blue in the face, with cold hands and embarrassed breathing. The Chinamen, in great excitement cried, " He die ! he die ! Take him out." His friend carried him out on the sidewalk, procured a carriage and took him home. There his friend informed Mr. D.'s wife that he had been drinking hard and nothing beyond that ailed him. He was too much frightened at his share in the business to call a physician, lest the whole thing should be discovered, and the young man was allowed to lie there, with little or nothing done for him, from 8 o'clock one night until 2 P.M. the following day. At this time he became conscious, called for a drink of whiskey, which he had no sooner swallowed than it came up, followed by a large quantity of blackish fluid. After this he felt greatly relieved and made a rapid recovery. This gentleman is now in the city and may be seen by any one wishing to verify this story.

The New York and Chicago papers contained an account, a few months ago, of a prostitute of the latter city, who had been on a spree, and who, going into a " joint " to smoke, dropped backward, dead, after a few inhalations. She is said to have had heart disease, and her death in this place may have been merely a coincidence.

A somewhat similar case, that of a young man, also said to have heart disease, occurred in a " joint " in Virginia City, Nevada.

From observing the symptoms that result from smoking opium I had thought that, possibly, codeia might be the active ingredient ; but when tried on a novice who had smoked once to excess, and on an old habitué, the first large doses produced no symp_ toms like those from smoking, and in the second twelve grains in no way appeased the desire for the pipe, nor delayed the unpleasant symptoms of abstinence. From six to eight grains of morphia would, however, take away all desire for the pipe, and prevent any unpleasant symptoms from arising. It is a curious fact that all smokers are extremely afraid of morphia, believing that if a man once gets to using it all hope of cure is out of the question.

Nausea, which is common in the case of the novice, is increased by the erect posture, walking, or by drinking any fluid. It is said by some that if the beginner will be very moderate (from one to four pipes) in his first few indulgences, he will not be troubled with nausea, or, if at all, not more than once or twice. Usually the novice, from the desire to show himself as strong as his companions,—sometimes because they lead him to smoke more than is good for him, and more often, perhaps, because he is disinclined to get up and leave his friends,—smokes to excess, and is consequently greatly nauseated. It seems to me very strange that this nausea, indicating a rebellion of the system against the poison, does not deter many from repeating the experiment. But it does not seem to do so. One of the hardest smokers that I ever knew—a man whom the pipe had ruined pecuniarily and socially, and whom I cured in a week's time—states that he was nauseated every day for the first five months of his addiction. Such blind disregard of nature's signals of distress is deserving of the evil consequences that follow.

The effect of smoking on the pulse of one addicted to the use of the drug is less marked, but bears, in the main, the characters just spoken of as resulting in the case of the novice. The pulse being usually dicrotic, increase in tension and lessening of frequency are well shown.

Old smokers do not, as is generally believed, smoke their few pipesful and then fall backward into a heavy sleep that is peopled by the most fantastic dreams and pleasing fancies. I am assured by some very intelligent Chinamen that the same may be said of their countrymen. It is not for the sleep that these people smoke, but for a condition of dreamy wakefulness that follows the smoking of their given amount. It is a state in which the devotee feels himself on a stratum above his fellow-men and their pursuits,—at peace with himself and all mankind,—a pleasant, listless calm and content-ment steals over him. Thus they dream,—disturbed —by any noise, angry at any interruption. This wak-ing dream, this silken garment of the imagination, will take its shape and its coloring from the most cherished and most brillant strands that are con-stantly running through the web and woof of their life's story. At one and the same time it puts out of sight the real and unpleasant crudities of daily life, and magnifies and elevates into view a pleasant bubble, whose play of colors and misty outlines are born of the pipe alone.

As the man's hopes, ambitions, aspirations, long-ings are, so will be the figures and incidents of his opium *dolce far niente.*

The pleasurable sensations, follow the first stage, or that of moderate exhilaration and talkativeness, vary in duration, according to the temperament of the individual and the amount of the drug used. Following it there may or may not be sleep. If the smoker has gone to excess a sleep sometimes follows, filled with the most horrible imagery and hallucinations, or a condition of wakefulness akin to that suffered by my nurse, Mr. K——. The following day the individual feels stupid and sleepy, this being banished, however, by a resort to the pipe again. The habitual smokers who do not use the drug to decided excess claim that, unlike any other manner of using opium, a headache the next day never follows.

It may not be amiss to say a few words further here, regarding the question of the production of sleep and stupor by opium-smoking, for upon nothing connected with the subject are such erroneous ideas held, even by travellers in China, from whom the masses have received their instructions. A few pipes taken with the "long draw," or full, deep inspiration, will produce sleep in the case of the novice, if he gives way to the feeling. Thus Surgeon Hill[1] describes a scene he witnessed on board the ship "Sunda": "The smoker, a young man of 24 years only, used eight pellets of the pea size, one after another, and all in the space of twenty minutes, making one long inspiration for each. He then fell into a profound sleep, which continued unbroken for three hours. The breathing was heavy and the circulation depressed, the pulsations being reduced about one in twenty."

[1] Quoted by Calkins, *op. cit.*, p. 52.

This man must have been a beginner, or an old smoker who was very sleepy from having lost rest previously. I have smoked eight, nay even sixteen such pipes, as have also my nurses, without feeling this necessity for sleep. The majority of the Chinese smokers do doze for hours after smoking; not because they smoke to decided excess or because they are forced to sleep, being overwhelmed by the narcotic, but, as they assure me, it is their way of pleasantly and indolently passing the time. When two or three are smoking together, conversation, and not sleep, is the rule. Amongst American smokers sleep immediately after and due to the smoking is an extremely rare condition. Calkins approaches the truth when he says: " The progress toward stupefaction is less speedy as experience grows into a habit. Old stagers may require hours and many repetitions ere the coveted excitation is reached." The majority of old smokers are not only not stupefied but complain that they are sleeping less than usual, their indulgence causing a distressing insomnia.

Enormous doses are sometimes smoked; quantities which if taken into the stomach would certainly produce death. To get nearly the same effect as from the pipe, a smoker who is daily consuming an ounce can pull through on 20 to 30 grains by the stomach, showing that but a small portion of the

active principle passes into the lungs with the smoke.
In the *Portfolio Chinensis* is mentioned the case of a
man who broke the habit, his daily dose by the pipe
being 1 tael (or 594 grains) daily, and who rapidly
improved in flesh and spirits afterward.   Libermann,
an attaché of the Imperial Army against the Yaous,
speaks of pellets of 6 grains in weight, 10, 20, 30, and
even 200 of these being used before the desired effect was produced.   He gives a tabulated statement of a thousand Chinese smokers of whom he
kept a record :

646	varied between	16 and 128	grains.
250	"	"	160 and 320	"
104	"	"	480 and 1,600	"

Surgeon Smith states that for the novice 5 grains
are sufficient, while he has known an old smoker to
go as high as 290 grains.

At the pauper-house, Singapore, Dr. Little as-
certained that of 15 persons, smokers for from 3 to
20, and averaging 11, years, the medium dose was 32
grains (Calkins).

I know one young lady in this city who, for some
time past, smoked 720 grains daily, and many who
smoke as high as 360 grains daily.   Some would use
more if they could afford it.   The case of the three
prostitutes who smoked over half a pound of opium
on a bet is unique in its way (see p. 73).

Rev. G. Smith, a missionary in China, found the average in 10 cases to be 1 *mace* (or 60 grains), and the general average to be 3 *candareens* (or 17½ grains)—(Allen-Calkins).

It will be seen from these figures that the average American smoker consumes as much, if not more, than the average Chinaman, and hence, if sleep or stupor followed in the one case as a direct result of the practice, we should expect to find it in the other, but we do not.

Did no ill effects, physical or mental, follow the prolonged or excessive use of the pipe, or did the pleasurable sensations always come with smoking, we could find in it a happiness and freedom from care that nothing else could give. Evil effects do follow, however, and that pleasant state of dreamy wakefulness fails, after a time, to respond, although large amounts are smoked. It may last a year, in rare cases two years, but more often only a few months. Then the good spirit of the pipe disappears, giving place to a demon who binds his victim hand and foot. Smoking no longer gives the pleasure of the first few months, and the victim to the habit continues not for the pleasure obtained from it, but driven to it by the terrible suffering that surely comes if the pipe is not smoked at the accustomed time. The pipe-habit resembles the other forms of the opium-habit in that :

1.   A gradual rise in the amount used is necessary in order to get the desired effect.

2.   The pleasurable symptoms that at first appear soon disappear.

3.   The evil effects on mind and body are alike in many respects ; and

4.   The symptoms incident to abstinence are the same.

Here is a description of a successful attempt to break off smoking at once, as described by a gentleman who had smoked twice daily for three years. It is interesting in many ways.

My dear Doctor :

At your request I give you a brief history of the manner in which I formed, broke, and relapsed into this accursed habit of smoking opium. As you say that you wish it for publication in your forthcoming articles, I must insist that no mention be made of my name, nor any clue given by which any one will surmise who I am, for God knows there is misery and degradation enough in the vice, and sufficient odium attaching to it, even amongst smokers, without publishing myself to the general public, and baring my miserable weakness to strangers. I write you, therefore, relying upon your good faith in this matter.

As you know, I am an actor, thirty-four years of age, and married. Three years ago, while playing in San Francisco, I was importuned by a friend to accompany him to a den in Chinatown where he was accustomed to smoke. To my sorrow I went, found several men and women there, smoking, was persuaded to try a few pipes, and from that day to this, with the exception of five months, have smoked steadily, usually twice a day. Although travelling from town to town I never had any difficulty in finding a place where opium was smoked, and in almost every place found a greater or less number of Americans smoking. Even in the little frontier towns of the West, a "joint" with opium and a full lay-out are to be found. Finding that I was becoming more firmly bound to this habit day by day, cursing the accident that first led me to the pipe, loathing the degradation of the thing, and being about to sail for Europe, I resolved to smoke for the last time. From 4 o'clock of the afternoon of the day I made that resolve I smoked until 1 o'clock the next day, and passed the gang-plank of the steamer minus any opiate. The first day I did very well, felt bright and buoyant, congratulated myself upon my resolve, and felt like informing my fellow-passengers what a bold dash I had made for the much-coveted freedom. I slept very well that night, but awoke at 4 A.M., sneezing, which came on in paroxysms, and was so severe that it shook me from crown to sole. Then I began to yawn and shiver. Cold chills crept up my back and down into my limbs ; flashes of heat alternated, seeming like fire by comparison. Nausea, accompanied by a dull, heavy headache, followed by vomiting and purging, then came on. So severe was the latter that it seemed as though I must remain on the stool all the time. By 8 P.M. I was in a pitiable condition ; the water was streaming from my burning eyes, the diarrhœa and vomiting persisted, extreme restlessness tormented me, and my whole body ached as if I had been beaten. During the night I saw the most horrible things. My valise, upon the floor, seemed to grow into the shape and size of an elephant ; strange faces peered at me from the dark corners and in unexpected places. I smelled the most horrible odors. Too weak to rise I vomited and purged in the bed. The surgeon who came to me left me some medicine, not knowing the cause of my suffering. The medicine had some preparation of opium in it, and I swallowed half the contents of the bottle, the dose of which was a teaspoonful, hoping that I might get enough opium to ease my suffering. Foolish hope, I threw it up as soon as it went down. I cursed my idiotic heroism in not bringing some opium with me, just in case of extreme illness like this. For the next two days a little iced champagne was all that I could retain ; sleep did not visit me ; the pains in my limbs, the sneezing and yawning persisted; and the horrible gloom of despair settled upon me like a pall. Had I been able to reach the deck I should have thrown myself overboard. As the days went on I mended somewhat, and when we reached port was able, with assistance, to walk to a carriage. It was fully six weeks before I left my hotel.

After a stay of five months in England I much improved in health and spirits,—another man in fact. I took the steamer for New York· Nearing the shores the old longing came back upon me with full force, and when I had reached the dock I sent my luggage to a hotel and made straight for a friendly " joint " in Mott Street. There the familiar faces, the old associations, the smell of the cooking opium, drove the memory of my struggle from my mind, and I determined to try just one pipe. The one became many, and from that hour I was as firmly bound to my hideous idol as ever. It is a sad parody on the strength of human resolve. I can say with Coleridge, as you quote him, " Oh, woful impotence of weak resolve ! " The old pleasure of the first year came to me only for a week or ten days ; then I sank into the same old never-ending rut. I am afraid that I can never again muster courage enough to break my bonds.

Those who have not smoked cannot understand the utter desolation that the habit works. Truly the name " fiend " is aptly used. It will make a villain of the best of men. There have been times when I believe that if I could not have obtained the money for opium otherwise, I would have taken the shoes from my wife's or child's feet and sold or pawned them.

Ah, well, the Dead Sea fruits are bitter.

Very truly yours, ———

P. S.   My daily average is $1.00 worth.[1]

Smokers generally do not seem to know that, like other forms of the opium habit, a single indulgence after a cure will in nine cases out of ten cause a relapse.

---

[1] About 230 grains.

There are some few, however, who, having been cured, find it possible to smoke occasionally without forming the habit.

After the receipt of this letter I saw this gentleman and asked him why he did not beg some opium from the doctor on board ship, and he replied that he could not tell why, save that the vomiting of the first medicine led him to believe that he could not retain it, and not having a pipe, and knowing nothing of the hypodermic method, he did not see how he could get any effect from it. Furthermore, he said that he was ashamed to acknowledge that he had been a smoker and was failing in an effort to abandon the habit. *

---

* Since writing this chapter and within a few days two opium-smokers, one a white man (the Mr. D. above referred to), the other a Chinaman, have died. Both died from the same cause, acute suppurative peritonitis, commonly known as inflammation of the bowels. Although opium was not the direct cause of death, the gastric and intestinal irritation, irregular eating, and marked constipation produced by it was undoubtedly the real, though remote, and certainly the predisposing cause of it.

CHAPTER V.

Some estimates—General effects of the practice—Misstatements and exaggerations by the over-zealous—A smoking match—Comparison with opium-eating—Danger of contracting syphilis.

BY the majority of smokers with whom I have talked regarding the prevalence of this habit amongst Americans, I have been told that my rough estimate of 6,000 falls far short of the actual number. Those who know the most about the matter are those theatrical people and travelling salesmen, who, having become slaves to the habit, make it their business to find out at every city or town at which they stop whether there are smoking-houses there, so that they may enjoy the companionship of others in their vice. I have never seen a smoker who found pleasure in using the drug at home and alone, no matter how complete his outfit, or how excellent his opium. These people, whom I have questioned closely, tell me that there is hardly a town of any size in the East, and none in the West, where there is not a place to smoke and Americans smoking. To be sure in many towns there is no regularly established opium-house, but there is always a Chinese laundry, the backroom of which serves the same purpose.

I was greatly amused one day not long since to see a traveling salesman who was going into a—to him—new region, get a letter of introduction from the keeper of a den in this city, which, when showed to a Chinaman anywhere, would procure him the means to indulge his opium appetite. Many habitual smokers when starting on a tour of acting, gambling, or selling goods, feel so certain that the implements and drug can be obtained at every place in which they stop that they take neither pipe nor opium with them.

The spread of this habit in this country has certainly been very rapid. I was lately talking with the party whom I have already instanced as being the second white man to smoke opium in the United States. Soon after his initiation he went to England, where he remained for a few months. On his return, he says, he was astonished to see the number who were smoking.

This is a vice that is certain to extend if it is not cut short by such measures as have been used against it in Nevada. Even then it is a question how far it can be limited, for there is a certain fascination about it, a certain element of good-fellowship, a pleasure in doing with some degree of secrecy that which the law forbids, and upon which the masses look as something mysterious, a curiosity on the part of the non-smoker to participate, and a decided pleasure amongst the habitués in making converts of their friends.

I have taken care to sift and verify the statements of the opium smokers, for they, like the morphia-takers, are prone to falsify in matters concerning their failing. Those statements only have been credited that came from men in different walks of life and from different parts of the country, and which proved to be the counterpart, the one of the other.

The question will be naturally asked, of what class are those who smoke opium? The answer is, representatives of all classes—merchants, actors, gentlemen of leisure, sporting men, telegraph operators, mechanics, ladies of good families, actresses, prostitutes, married women, and single girls. Those who have the most leisure, those on whose hands time hangs heavily, are the most prone to drift into it, and be carried away by it. Essentially a nervous people, prone to go to excess in every thing, gladly welcoming narcotics and stimulants, we go to very decided excess in all matters of this kind. As an example of foolhardy excess take the following, which I have upon good authority: A purse of $50 was made up for three prostitutes in San Francisco, the whole to go to that one who smoked the most opium in a given time. It took about thirty hours of steady smoking before the matter was decided, when it was found that the three had consumed $13 worth of opium, the winner having smoked over $5 worth. At the rate at which opium was then selling this would have represented over half a pound for the three, and 3¼ oz., or 1,560 grains, for the winner. She paid dearly for her victory, being taken quite ill and confined to her bed for over a month.

It must not be supposed that all Chinamen or all Americans who smoke smoke to excess. Some, especially the former, smoke but once a week. As in the case of opium- or morphia-takers, there are rare instances where persons smoke the pipe for months without forming any habit, and without any apparent injury to either mind or body.

A very odd conceit obtains with many smokers. When you ask them, "Can you stop this?" they will answer with the utmost assurance, especially if they have been smoking for an hour or two and are well primed with opium: "Stop it? Certainly. For instance, this will be my last smoke for a month." Nevertheless, you will find him there smoking as usual the next day, and for many days thereafter. Some men will bid their companions good-night and good-bye night after night, sometimes for months, about as follows: " Well, boys, good-bye. I 've had my last smoke with you. It has given me a world of pleasure and served to while away many a tedious hour, and I forgive it whatever harm it's done me. I wish you joy. Good-bye." The next night he will be found smoking again as hard as ever, and at the finish go through the same performance.

The women who are to be found smoking at the joints manifest no bashfulness in smoking with strange men, and evince no hesitation in going down into the slums to meet other habitués. They usually remove the shoes, loosen the corsets, and remain for hours on the hard wooden bunks.

It has been found that in China the evil effects of smoking opium manifest themselves sooner and more powerfully upon the poorer classes. This has been ascribed to the fact that they are insufficiently fed and clothed, and are less able to withstand the inroads of the poison. The fact that they chiefly smoke the dregs, and the dregs of the dregs, must also be taken into consideration. I have noticed that amongst those American smokers whose means permit them to live well the ill effects are delayed the longest. Between opium-smoking and chronic alcoholism there can be no comparison. The latter is by far the greater evil, both as regards its effects on the individual and on the community. The opium-smoker does not break furniture, beat his wife, kill his fellow-men, reel through the streets disgracing himself or friends, or wind up a long debauch comatose in the gutter. He is not unfitted for work to the same extent that an inebriate is. True organic lesions rarely follow.

Many Chinamen smoke, and we should expect to find them incapacitated for work by it. But it is not so. From the overwhelming testimony given before the Congressional Committee [1] to the effect that Chinamen, placed side by side with American, Irish, and British miners, do more than they in a given time on the hardest kind of work, we are fain to believe that the extreme physical deterioration claimed to result from opium-smoking must need some modification before being admitted to full belief.

I have lately received from London a little book containing a series of twelve plates, taken from the Chinese, illustrating the fall, through opium-smoking, of a rich Chinese merchant from affluence and honor to poverty, degradation, and, finally, death. It is unquestionably an exaggeration. For, though no one questions the ill effects of opium-smoking, we cannot believe, with our present knowledge, that the subject of these plates is a type of all smokers. I know men, Americans and Chinese, who are in this city to-day and can be seen, who have been hard smokers for ten years, and who present none of the features usually ascribed to the smoker. Two,

---

[1] Seward: Chinese Immigration, etc., N. Y., 1881.

in particular, are of magnificent muscular development.

There are those in California, however, who think that amongst the American smokers there the ill effects are very decided. Thus, a writer in the *San Jose Mercury* (Oct. 8, 1881), in condemning the pictures of Thulstrup, who illustrated my first article in *Harper's Weekly*, says:

The tremulous hand, the vacant expression, preternatural[1] paleness, the spasm, the convulsive clutch, the apathy lethargy, the sudden swoon, the inordinate craving, the now excited brain, the vain babbling, the waking with a sudden shriek, the imagined pursuers, the terrors of ten million remembered minute expressions repeated unceasingly, reacted over and over again ; the waste and tear of tissue, fibre, brain ; the lack of appetite, the inordinate craving for a repugnant poison, the inexpressible drowsiness of the *yen-yen-g-fun ;* the bitter consciousness of a million unperformed duties ; the gradual weakness, mental, physical impotency, positive, if persisted in ; insanity, frequent or sudden death.

The whitened, blanched faces of prematurely old youth, the dark-circled eye, the nerveless look, the unsteady gait, the unquenchable look of a fatal desire, the thin white hand,—are already seen among us.

In the great city of San Francisco, boys, yes and girls, with the look of cunning, blasé old men and women, sneak out of vile alleys in the Chinese quarter and elsewhere,—out into the beautiful sunshine and refreshing sea-breeze, with such expression of weariness, duplicity, vice, and recklessness combined on every face, that the busy passer-by stops to pity and abhor.

The foolish, misguided, crazy boy—deceiving father, mother, and

---

[1] This would imply that the person is naturally pale, the vice making him pale.

employer—who deems it something smart and clever to "visit a joint," or "to hit the flute." The poor young fool stifles both conscience and his nostrils, and pretends to look approvingly and with the eye of a connoisseur on the box of deadly poison, and holding in the flame the dirty bowl charged with the prepared, perforated ball, draws death, dishonor, and disease in one fatal inhalation eagerly into his system. It is the road to speedy decay and rapid dissolution. An idolatry that has slain more thousands than Juggernaut. It is the curse of China. An impending evil that, transplanted here, if not rooted out, would, before the dawn of another century, decimate our youth, emasculate the coming generation, if not completely destroy the white population of our coast.

This pernicious habit is on the increase, of late, all over this State, especially in the large cities. Many bright young men, including two, at least, graduates of our universities, have died from its effects within the past year. The police records of San Francisco show the arrest of hundreds of both sexes annually—many of them youth of respectable exterior—in the vilest of Chinese "joints." Opium-smoking, in ninety-nine cases out of a possible hundred, means the mad-house or the morgue, and not far off, either.

The intention of this writer, who signs himself as Burt Hale, is unquestionably good ; but he makes a grave mistake, made by so many others who have written in the same tone upon this subject, *i. e.*, that of saying a great deal that is untruthful and exaggerated, knowing it to be so, and hoping thus to so work upon the feelings of the reader as to disgust him with the subject and prevent his being led into temptation. I firmly believe that such a course does more harm than good in the majority of cases, the plain, unvarnished truth, each statement of which is susceptible of actual proof and based on facts, working the most good in the long run. Many who read, and happen, despite the warning, to try the pipe, and find its effects unlike those described, gather from the habitués and see with their own eyes that the statements regarding the mad-house and the morgue is absurd, will conclude that every thing else that has been written by the same author is untruthful.

There is much in Burt Hale's remarks that is based on facts and that points a very forcible moral. The danger of contracting that loathsome disease, syphilis, from the pipe-stem that has passed from mouth to mouth a hundred times a day for months and years is, as Burt Hale states it, real, and a fact that should make the smoker hesitate before accepting the instrument from the hands of chance smoking-acquaintances. With the class who smoke this disease is especially frequent. I know of one instance where a respectable young man, a telegraph operator, thus contracted a syphilitic chancre of the lip that was followed by the horde of destroying symptoms that usually result. He had to throw up his situation, and barely escaped with his life. Two other cases, one an American, the other a Chinaman, have since come under my care.

A Chinese scholar,[1] quoted by Williams,[2] thus

---

[1] Chinese Repository, vol. vii, p. 108.   [2] The Middle Kingdom, etc.

sums up the ill effects of opium, which, he says, is taken first to raise the animal spirits and prevent lassitude.

"It exhausts the animal spirits, impedes the regular performance of business, wastes the flesh and blood, dissipates every kind of property, renders the person ill-favored, promotes obscenity, discloses secrets, violates the laws, attacks the vitals, and destroys life." And again : " In comparison with arsenic, I pronounce it tenfold the greater poison ; one swallows arsenic because he has lost his reputation and is so involved that he cannot extricate himself. Thus driven to desperation he takes the dose and is destroyed at once ; but those who smoke the drug are injured in many ways. It may be compared to raising the wick of a lamp, which, while it increases the blaze, hastens the exhaustion of the oil and extinction of the light. Hence, the youth who smoke will shorten their own days, and cut off all hope of posterity, leaving their parents and wives without any one on whom to depend. From the robust who smoke the flesh is gradually consumed and worn away, and the skin hangs like a bag. Their faces become cadaverous and black, and their bones naked as billets of wood. The habitual smokers doze for days over their pipes, without appetite ; when the desire for opium comes on they cannot resist its impulse. Mucus flows from their nostrils and tears from their eyes ; their bodies are rotten and putrid. * * * * The poor smoker who has pawned every article in his possession still remains idle ; and when the periodical thirst comes on, will even pawn his wives and sell his daughters. In the province of Ngauhwui I once saw a man named Chin, who being childless, purchased a concubine, and got her with child ; afterward, when his money was expended and other means all failed him, being unable to resist the desire for the pipe, he sold her in her pregnancy for several tens of dollars. This money being expended he went and hung himself. Alas ! how painful was his end."

Williams [1] says that about twelve ordinary pipes daily, or about as

---

[1] *Op. cit.,* p. 391.

much opium as will balance a franc piece, can seldom be exceeded without decided ill effects. "Two mace weight taken daily is considered an immoderate dose, which few can bear for any length of time ; and those who are afraid of the effect of the drug upon themselves endeavor not to exceed a mace (60 grains). Some persons who have strong constitutions and stronger resolutions continue the use of the drug within these limits for many years without disastrous effects upon their health and spirits, though most of even these moderate smokers are so much the slaves of the habit that they feel too wretched, nerveless, and imbecile to go on with their business without the stimulus.

"The testimony regarding the evil effects of the use of this pernicious drug, which deserves better to be called 'an article of destruction ' than an ' article of luxury,' is so unanimous that few can be found to stand up strongly in its favor. Dr. Smith, a physician in charge of the hospital at Penang, says : ' The baneful effects of this habit on the human constitution are particularly displayed by stupor, forgetfulness, general deterioration of all the mental faculties, emaciation, debility, sallow complexion, lividness of lips and eyelids, languor and lack-lustre of eye, and appetite either destroyed or depraved, sweetmeats or sugar being the articles that are most relished.' "

As compared with other ways of using the drug habitually, there is no question in my mind but that in smoking (1) it takes longer to form a real habit, (2) it works less physical and mental injury when once formed, and (3) it is much easier to cure.

Take the following as an example : A young man who had been smoking steadily for two years tried the substitution of pills of cooked smoking-opium by the mouth, with the result of losing eighteen pounds in flesh in three week's time and destroying all appetite for food. He returned to the pipe, when the digestive disturbances disappeared, and he rapidly regained the flesh he had lost.

Upon the morals, however, the pipe-habit exercises a very strong influence. The surroundings, the low companionship, and the effect of the drug, combine to effect any thing other than a raising of the moral tone. Female smokers, if not already lost in point of virtue, soon become so.

Financially, the habit has but one tendency, viz., ruin, not so much from the money expended on the drug (from 50c. to $3.00 per day) as from neglect of business and the impaired mental power brought to bear upon it for the short time that it receives any attention.

Ho-King-Shan says, according to Calkins: " For the wasting of time and dissipation of means, and the moral depravation of the man besides, the opium-pipe is without its rival." Sir C. Forbes writes: "For fascinating seductiveness, immeasurable agony, and appalling ruin, the world has yet to see its parallel." And Barnes: " Not the reptile, with its fascinating eye, draws the impotently fluttering bird so surely within its gaping jaws. Opium is a spirit of evil as treacherously beguiling as is the Arch-fiend himself."

A hard smoker will spend the greater part of the

day in smoking, and consequently can devote but little time to his business or his family.   It is a slow and tedious process,—cooking and puffing,—and as some "fiends" must consume enormous quantities to get any effect, it takes time.   If the companion-ship is pleasant and the subjects of conversation interesting, time flies very rapidly.

CHAPTER VI.

Effects of opium-smoking on the different systems, organs, and apparatuses.

I propose in this place to analyze and classify the effects of opium-smoking upon the individual in the same manner that I did those of opium, morphine, and chloral-taking in my work, "Drugs That Enslave," believing that in this manner a more just appreciation and careful study of the ill effects of the vice may be obtained than by loose generalization and weak moralizing. My observations have been limited to a general study of some thirty, and a special study of twelve, cases of this habit. Some of the habitués came directly to my house and permitted me to study and experiment upon them for six and eight hours at a time, both while smoking and when not having smoked for some hours. I have also had in my home, for treatment, one gentleman who was a smoker and morphia-taker at the same time, and three who were very heavy smokers. I have thus been enabled to obtain considerable interesting and reliable information, which, when combined with the experiments made upon my nurses and myself, fill out the picture very well. From books and from other physicians I have obtained almost nothing of importance, owing to the fact that this habit, especially amongst Americans, has never been studied at all scientifically.

The Mind. It is upon the mind first that we see the decided effects of opium-smoking. With the novice and the commencing habitué, pleasant exhilaration, followed by lazy insouciance, contentment, a feeling of perfect rest, with development of one's benevolent qualities, are apparent. A step further and we get less true exhilaration and more of the waking-dream. After smoking from three months to a year, the pleasurable sensations gradually cease to respond, though the amount of opium smoked is largely increased. Surprised and disgusted the victim abandons the pipe, but for a short time only, for when the customary time for indulgence comes the victim finds that he is no longer drawn to his habit with silken cords, but that he is *compelled* to return to it. The shackles that he has lazily and indolently riveted upon himself now refuse to be unloosed, and he finds himself bound to an idol that he despises. The first effects of smoking upon the mind of the habitué are disinclination for continued mental effort, weakening of the will power, wavering in decision, and loss of memory. Thus, those actors and singers who smoke, not only find it difficult to commit their lines to memory, but even when well committed they will sometimes suddenly elude the grasp and leave nothing but a blank behind.

There is often a gloom that takes possession of the person, a feeling of impending evil that can only be dissipated by a further recourse to the pipe.

In the smallest action of the habitué, especially after smoking, there is a certain indecision, reflected in the face by a childish perplexity and impatience.

There is sometimes a failure to coördinate ideas. Excessive smoking, even in an old habitué, will sometimes produce a condition of mind analogous to that of the nurse whose case is described at p. 54. There is a dread of going to sleep, lest something happens, and sleep, when it does come, is not restful or refreshing, but filled with a succession of horrible phantasmagoria.

The will power is weakened or destroyed. There is a tendency to falsify without any reason for so doing. As to the production of actual insanity by the excessive smoking of opium, I can learn of but few cases amongst white smokers. One such case is that of a young man in San Francisco, æt. 31, known as "Footsey." He seems to have been a catspaw for gamblers and a runner for the inmates of houses of ill repute, having no regular home or fixed means of subsistence. It is said by some that he was sound enough, mentally, until he commenced smoking opium, when he rapidly went to pieces, and was sent to the Napa City Asylum for the Insane. Others claim that opium-smoking had nothing to do with his insanity, he having used the pipe for but a few months and then irregularly. I have written three times to the Napa Asylum, but have received no reply, as yet. In the absence of any more definite information the case is worthy only of passing mention.

Dr. Shurtleff, of the Stockton Asylum, writes that he can give me no definite statistics regarding the number of Chinese that have entered the State Asylum, in whose cases opium-smoking was the cause of insanity. That it does produce this condition, however, he is certain, having had several cases under treatment.

The following statistics from the California State Insane Asylum, go to show that insanity amongst the Chinese is not very common either from opium-smoking or from any other cause.

	NO. OF INSANE CHINESE.
1865	9
1866	10
1867	8
1868	10
1869	17

NO. OF INSANE CHINESE.

1870	.	.	.	.	. 13
1871	.	.	.	.	. 13
1872	.	.	.	.	. 24
1873	.	.	.	.	. 16
1874	.	.	.	.	. 23
1875	.	.	.	.	. 27

Mr. Seward, from whose able and very interesting work the foregoing table is taken, says:[1] "Taking the table of the State Insane Asylum, we find that in 1860 there were seven Chinese inmates out of two hundred and forty-eight, and in 1870, thirteen out of five hundred and sixty-two. The difference in the percentage in this direction is so great as to occasion surprise, more particularly when one remembers that the absence of women has a direct and positive tendency to increase forms of vice which occasion insanity."

In a letter just received from Dr. Shurtleff, he says:

Up to Nov. 15, 1875, when a new State Asylum was opened at Napa, all the insane of our State had been kept in this institution. That year we had had an average of 40 Chinese patients. The Chinese in this State are not averse to sending their people to the asylum for the insane, and they are generally committed as soon as they become dangerous or burdensome.

I estimate the Chinese population at that time (1875) in California at 65,000. This gives us about 1 insane Chinese person to every 1,625 of the Chinese population. The Workingmen's Party, or "Sand-lot" agitators, extravagantly estimated the number of Chinese in the

---

[1] Chinese Immigration in its Social and Economical Aspects, N. Y., 1881.

State much greater at that time. I have not the census returns of 1880 at hand.

The ratio of all the insane in California at the same time was about 1 insane person to every 500 of the whole general population, estimating the number of the insane by the number in the Asylum. I should have said above, that not only was the average number of Chinese patients in 1875 about 40, but that the average was also about 40 for the decade from 1870 to 1880.

The tenth census returns will show a much larger ratio of insanity in our State than I have here given, based upon the number in our Asylum up to 1875, in part, because the insane of the State of Nevada and of the Territory of Arizona are kept, and were enumerated, in California ; and in part, because absolutely *all* the insane are never under asylum care, though they come exceptionally near it in this State.

I have observed two forms of insanity in the Chinese opium-smoker, falling under the two general classes termed *dementia* and *acute mania.* These dements are extremely emaciated, weak, and degraded in appearance, the result, presumably, of protracted habit. They generally improve under asylum treatment, but they do not fully recover. In the other class, the mania is characterized by constant maniacal excitement, a wild, haggard look, an incoherent, rambling loquacity, delusions, hallucinations, sleeplessness, etc. Recovery may take place in these cases if the patient does not die early of exhaustion. The cause of the mental disorder in these cases, I suppose to be a temporary excess, rather than a protracted habit in opium-smoking—an opium-smoking debauch, or spree.

I have also had among the Chinese patients many cases of *simple melancholia, acute melancholia with delusions* of *danger* and *persecution*, and *melancholia attonita;* but, as I stated in my former letter, the statistics of the causes of the insanity of the Chinese patients are too defective for scientific use.

No patients belonging to the white races, whose insanity was attributed to opium-smoking, have, *as yet* been committed to this asylum, but they will come.

I have had under my own care, during more than sixteen years in this Institution, in all 256 Chinese patients. We have now only 34. The whole number of patients in the Institution of all races being to-day just 1,100.

Since Nov. 15, 1875, more Chinese have been sent to the Napa Asylum than to this,—that being nearer San Francisco.

The percentage of the really insane amongst opium- and morphine-consumers is not large, and with smokers, like the former, while we should expect to find moral insanity, or rather *moral weakness*, true intellectual insanity is probably rarely met with. The mental aspect of a confirmed smoker, however, is any thing but pleasing. There is dullness, apathy, disinclination for mental effort of any kind, groundless fear, weakness, and vacillation, outbursts of violent temper, proneness to falsify, and the like, all of which make themselves manifest on the face of the victim. He looks completely "dragged out," and as though nothing short of an earthquake could disturb the continued mental hebetude.

Suicide may be committed during a fit of despondency, especially by women and young girls. One such case occurred in this city lately. A young woman, a smoker of about one year's standing, handed her jewelry to two friends who were with her and deliberately threw herself from the pier into the river. She was rescued, and has not since made the attempt to destroy herself.

As most of the female smokers are prostitutes, and as attempts at self-destruction are not uncommon amongst this class, this is not surprising and need not be laid at the door of opium. Those who are not prostitutes, and who having smoked, are led astray, have an evident cause, other than opium, for such acts.

Delirium tremens, either acute or chronic, a not uncommon result of the excessive hypodermic use of morphine, has never, to my knowledge, resulted from opium-smoking.

The Nervous System.—The effects upon the nervous system are not so marked as in the case of opium-eating or the hypodermic use of morphine. Neuralgias are rare. Occasionally neuralgia of the bowels is complained of, but I question whether it is not due to colic from flatus, incidental to irregular eating, imperfect digestion, and constipation, more than to opium.

Tremor of isolated muscles sometimes occurs. If the person is pursuing the practice to very decided excess, general tremor—most marked in the hands and tongue—is seen. These people may be classed under the very loose, yet expressive term "nervous." They start at any sudden noise or loud sound, and seem irritated and unstrung by that which, to a person in health, would pass unnoticed. Epileptiform convulsions and paralysis, although often spoken of by lay writers, do not occur.

Eyes.—The pupils are, as a rule, evenly con-tracted. Conjunctivitis, with burning and excessive lachrymation, is not unusual. When the effect of the last dose has worn off and the demand for more of the drug is felt, the pupils will often be found widely dilated. All who have smoked the drug for any length of time complain that they are getting near-sighted.

In the novice, in addition to myosis, the eyes ap-pear swollen or " bunged up," as though one had been drinking, or had passed a sleepless night. There is also a sensation as though there was sand in the eyes, and the skin of the forehead feels stiff and drawn. Dark circles often form beneath the eye.

Circulation.—The pulse is usually above the nor-mal, save after excessive smoking, when in the course of several hours, the temporary acceleration is replaced by a fall below the usual rate.

Thus, in eighteen observations on six persons it was found that the rule was for the pulse rate to rise in the first two hours in frequency, with a slight rise in tension ; to fall in from two to three hours to the customary, with tension stationary and a shortened up-stroke ; and to rise in frequency, tension, and height of up-stroke in the following twelve hours.

For example.

W. H., æt. 30, no heart trouble, has smoked for 4 years.

PULSE.

Before smoking. Has not smoked for 20 hours	80	High up-stroke—dicrotic.
After smoking 10 pipes . . .	94-106	Shortened up-stroke. Tidal wave $\frac{3}{10}$ above base line.
After smoking 16 " . . .	118	Up-stroke stationary. Tidal wave $\frac{5}{10}$ above base line.
Three hours after smoking . .	94	Same.
Six hours after " . . .	68	Up-stroke raised $\frac{2}{10}$. Tidal wave has fallen $\frac{4}{10}$.
Twenty hours after " . . .	120	High up-stroke. Hyperdicrotic and irregular in rhythm.

In an extremely nervous subject with a rapid (100) pulse at the start there are produced increase in tension and decided lessening of rapidity (72).

In some excessive smokers twenty pipes seem to exercise no influence on the frequency of the pulse beyond raising the tension a little.

Flushing of the face and profuse perspiration occurs in the case of the novice after a few pipes. In an old and hard smoker the countenance attains a sallow, corpse-like hue.

The effect on the pulse of a novice has already been spoken of.

The Urinary Organs.—The average specific gravity of the urine of a smoker is low (1,004 to 1,016); the reaction is usually neutral; the odor normal; the color a pale straw or amber; microscopically, mucus fibrillæ and a few epithelial cells; chemically, an actual increase in the earthy and alkaline phosphates; no albumen or sugar (in 20 examinations), and morphia in varying quantity *always.*

Difficulty in making water, both in the case of the novice and the old smoker, is usually found. In the male there seems to be a blunting of the sensibility, with spasm of the deep urethral muscles. There is difficulty in getting started, the wait being sometimes as long as three or four minutes, with occasional stopping of the stream, evidently due to spasm, every few moments.

In the female there is no such spasm and the irritability of the bladder seems to be increased.

The Sexual Organs.—For the first few months of smoking there is, in both the male and the female, considerable erethrism, in spite of which, however, completion of the act is markedly delayed. After a time, however, both desire and power are materially impaired. This is most noticeable immediately after smoking. I have already spoken of the disgraceful conduct of some smokers in getting innocent girls to smoke in order to excite their passions and effect their ruin.

In some few women menstruation is stopped, not to return until the habit is broken. In the majority, however, it is either rendered scanty and irregular, or, as in most cases, is not interfered with at all. In this it differs materially from the morphia-habit, especially that by hypodermic injection.

The children of American smokers, so far as can be learned, are strong and healthy. Some women who smoke to excess miscarry frequently. Well-authenticated cases are known here where children have been born to man and wife who were both old smokers. A Scotchman with whom I am well acquainted, and who has been a hard smoker for the past six or eight years, has just been presented with a fine little girl.

On abandoning the habit seminal emissions occur, as when other forms of the habit are broken.

That opium-smoking, like morphia-taking, exercises a decided influence upon the procreative power of the Chinese people must be inferred from the statistics of their increase in population, which statistics, though unreliable in many ways, are sufficiently accurate as to the ratio of increase to prove the point advanced. Thus :

From 1711 to 1753 the population increased 74,222,602, which was an annual advance of 1,764,824, or a little more than 6 per cent. per annum for 42 years. This high rate, it must be remembered, does not take into account the more thorough subjugation of the South and West at the later date when the Manchus could safely enrol large districts where in 1711 they would not have been permitted to enter for such a purpose.

From 1752 to 1792 the increase was 104,636,882, or an annual advance of 2,682,997 inhabitants, or about 2½ per cent. per annum for 39 years. During this period the country enjoyed almost uninterrupted peace, under the vigorous sway of Kievlung, and the unsettled regions of the South and West rapidly filled up.

From 1792 to 1812 the increase was 54,126,679, or an annual advance of 2,706,333, not quite one per cent. per annum for twenty years.[1]

As opium-smoking was in full operation between 1735 and 1812, as there were no other factors of importance tending to modify materially the percentage of increase in population, we are forced to the conclusion that this vice has had much to do with the rapidly falling percentage of population increase,— a fall from six to a little less than one per cent. in 100 years. It is a curious fact that it has been urged as an argument in favor of England's continuing the opium trade with China, that smoking is a benefit to this overcrowded land, in that the practice of this vice materially limits the number of children born.[2]

From observations made on American and Chinese smokers, male and female, in this country, the effect of opium-smoking as a destroyer or modifier of procreative power is not very decided,—not so marked as in morphia-takers. Still, in China, where more of the drug is smoked, and the dregs chiefly by the poor, who form the largest class of smokers, the effect may be more apparent.

---

[1] Williams, *op. cit.*
[2] Davidson, " Trade and Travel."

Alimentary Canal.—Upon the digestive tract the effect is the same, although usually in a less degree, as when the drug is taken by the skin or mouth, viz., loss of appetite, some gastric catarrh, and constipation. Incident to the constipation are piles, sometimes accompanied by obstinate itching about the anus There is often a craving for sweet things. The secretions are, as a rule, checked. A violent attack of diarrhœa, merging into a chronic condition, which lasts for weeks or months, sometimes supervenes upon the constipation.

The vomiting that attacks the novice is peculiar, and in some cases very distressing. It is excited by the erect posture, walking, or drinking water. Smokers believe that if the novice drinks tea that vomiting will not result. This is not so. In the majority of instances the vomiting is sudden and unexpected, and consists in a simple spasmodic emptying of the stomach. In some cases, however, the nausea and vomiting occur every time the person smokes for from one to six months, and, as in my own case, the nausea may persist for forty-eight hours, and the vomiting be so violent as to strain the person and eventuate in the raising of blood and a bile-tinged mucus.

The Respiratory Tract. — Prolonged smoking usually produces a low grade of bronchitis, with slight cough, pharyngeal and laryngeal catarrh, with loss of power in the vocal cords. This is particularly distressing to actors and singers. They should never smoke before commencing their night's work. Catarrh of the throat and nose are occasionally troublesome. That the effect upon the throat is very decided is proven by the fact that in the majority of cases a dull, aching, drawing sensation in the pharynx and larynx is one of the first symptoms of abstinence.

The Cutaneous Surface.—The habitual smoker is marked by a pallid, sometimes sallow complexion; more often the former in the case of Americans. Herpes and other trophic changes are rare. It has been found that the perspiration of smokers, which is sometimes profuse, stains the body and bed-linen of a brownish color, and has an odor of opium. In some old smokers, so intense is the itching, especially of the genitals, that they excoriate themselves by persistent scratching. The genitals of one smoker with whom I am acquainted are a mass of sores thus produced and perpetuated. With some, itching is rarely felt, even though the smoking be excessive. It is produced or aggravated by warmth, as the heat of summer, or when well covered up in bed.

Locomotion and Coördination.—Irregularity of gait and the like, most marked after smoking to excess, are due to the production of a "dazed" condition of mind, rather than to any direct effect on the muscular system.

Intermittent Fever.—I know of but one case where malarial symptoms of a well-marked type could be attributed to the smoking of opium. Change of residence, large doses of quinine, arsenic, eucalyptus, and iodine produced no effect. Rapid reduction of the daily allowance of opium (all other medicine having been stopped) caused a disappearance of all symptoms. To test the matter, the full daily allowance was after a few weeks again resorted to, with the result of bringing back the symptoms again, the quotidian, however, having been changed to a tertian type.

CHAPTER VII.

Symptoms of abstinence—Proportion of relapses—Relative ease of cure—Manner of treating.

THE symptoms that follow the sudden abandonment of the pipe are precisely the same as those that are incident to the deprivation of morphia or opium when used by the month or hypodermically. The only difference is, possibly, one of degree, the smoker suffering less severely and for a shorter time than the opium- or morphia-taker The respiratory tract and eyes, however, with which the opium-smoke comes in direct contact, are affected out of proportion to the rest of the body. There seems to be a local as well as a general reaction. The intestinal colic, too, is of a somewhat different character from that which results from the morphia- or opium-taker's abstinence.

The first symptoms are gaping, yawning, sneezing, a discharge of tears and mucus from the eyes and nose, irregularity of the pupils, ringing in the ears, followed by extreme restlessness, nausea, vomiting, and purging. There may be almost constant vomiting, and also from 20 to 40 passages

from the bowels in 24 hours.   Chills chase each
other along the spine, followed by flashes of heat
and profuse perspiration.   A peculiar, dry, drawing,
burning pain in the throat, and tearing pains, most
marked in the calves of the legs, in the loins, and
between the shoulders, are felt.   These pains are
usually very distressing in the worst cases.   If no
opiate is used and the vomiting and diarrhœa continue, the restlessness and flushed face give place to
quiet, with paleness, sunken eyes, collapse, and
death.   When not going to this extreme, or when
the proper remedies are used, the person slowly returns to a normal condition, the distressing and
dangerous symptoms abating one by one.   Sleeplessness usually persists for a long time.   As time
goes on the pains in the limbs gradually fade away;
seminal emissions in the male and sexual desire in
the female show themselves; the appetite returns
and becomes ravenous; weight is gained and the
natural buoyancy of spirit shows itself.   Bronchitis and catarrh of the throat, if the person has
been a heavy smoker, usually persists for months.

These, then, are the sufferings endured by those
who pass through the ordeal wholly unassisted by
baths and medicine.   Under proper treatment the
suffering is really very little.   The majority of
those who try to break themselves, seldom carry the
struggle to a successful issue.

In China the natives suffer in the same manner.

" The thirst and burning sensation in the throat, which the wretched sufferer feels, only to be removed by a repetition of the dose, which proves one of the strongest links in the chain that drags him to his ruin. At this stage of the habit, his case is almost hopeless ; if the pipe be delayed too long, vertigo, complete prostration, and discharge of water from the eyes ensue ; if entirely withheld, coldness and aching pains are felt over the body, an obstinate diarrhœa supervenes, and death closes the scene." [1]

To one who has treated many cases of the morphia- or opium-habit, where the drug has been used by the mouth or subcutaneously, the management and speedy cure of the opium-smoker seems a very easy matter. For instance : When I first began to investigate this subject I picked out the hardest case to be found among the opium-smokers in this city,—a man who had ruined himself financially, mentally, morally, and physically by the practice,— one who was looked upon by all the smokers in the East, West, and South (for he was known and had smoked almost everywhere) as the greatest of all " opium fiends." I offered to cure him for nothing, if he would let me try. He would scrape the bowl and eat the ash ; would steal it from the Chinamen ;

---

[1] Williams, *op. cit.*, p. 393.

would pawn his wife's clothing for opium. He was in the De Quincey Home just four days and under treatment but ten. He was broken of his habit thus speedily and effectually with almost no suffering,—nothing as compared to what an ordinary smoker would suffer in breaking himself. After leaving me he gained very rapidly in flesh, and is to-day free from the vice and has absolutely no craving for the drug. He had been a hard smoker for from eight to ten years. Others that I have since treated have gone through in the same easy and rapid manner. I hope in a few days to be able to persuade a Chinaman who has been smoking for the past twenty-eight years, and who is said to be the hardest smoker in the city, to let me cure him.

The first patient—the American "fiend"—had once experienced the horrors of sudden deprivation on shipboard, and did not believe, until it was proved to him, that a comparatively painless and rapid cure was possible.

This treatment consists in the use of capsicum, digitalis, and cannabis Indica tincture in large doses, often repeated. The bromides of potassium and sodium, if there is much reflex nervous trouble, may be given. The bromides should be administered in 100 gr. doses twice daily, *in plenty of water,*[1] as then their absorption is more full and

---

[1] The physiological and therapeutical action of the bromide of potassium and bromide of ammonium. E. H. Clark and R. Amory, Boston, 1874.

rapid. Their use, however, should be continued for only a few days at the most.

In addition to this, bismuth and catechu in large doses for the diarrhœa and vomiting; chloride of gold and soda, ½ gr. every two hours in the form of pill or Fuller's tablets, with fl. ext. gelseminum, to relieve the pains in the limbs; massage and electro-massage, hot baths and cold spray for the same purpose; oxide of zinc and atropia for the profuse perspiration; and hyoscyamus and chloral to produce sleep; stimulants, of which iced champagne is the best, should be freely used for 48 *hours only.*

Later, to relieve dryness of the throat, fl. extract of jaborandi; muriate of ammonia, and benzoic acid for the bronchitis, and nitrate of silver for the pharyngitis, prove of service. Tonics, short warm baths with cold douche or spray, phosphorus and cod-liver oil, and out-door exercise, are all called for. Some occupation should be engaged in that does not leave too much leisure time, and a course of reading pursued and associations cultivated that tend to elevate the mental and moral tone of the individual.

Opium-smokers, like opium- and morphine-takers, can only be reliably and satisfactorily treated in an institution where they can be watched and restrained day and night for at least two weeks.[1]

---

[1] More exact directions for treatment may be found in " Drugs That Enslave," etc., Philadelphia, 1881.

A longer stay, when possible, is always advisable, for then an opportunity is given for thoroughly building up the system and allowing the individual to regain moral and mental tone, without which relapse is sure to occur.

In the case of those who use the drug by the mouth or hypodermically, after-treatment is still more important, as it is necessary to watch for and combat the return of the disease for which the drug was originally taken legitimately. The opium-smoker has no such excuse of pain to drive him to his vice. He voluntarily and knowingly drifts into a habit, the undercurrent of which is sure to carry him beyond his depth and draw to him down.

From the meagre statistics at hand it is impossible to say what proportion of smokers who have abandoned the habit, relapse.

As time passes, the memory of the agonizing struggle for freedom from the vice fades, and the former smoker, either from a morbid craving for some narcotic or stimulant, or from evil association, tries a single pipe, with the result of again firmly fixing himself in the clutches of his old enemy.

There are quacks in the West who put up medicine which will, they claim, enable a smoker to abandon the pipe without suffering. It is a cunning bait, but a delusive one, it having led many to ruin; for containing some preparation of opium or morphine, they often fix the victim in the double habit of smoking and taking the drug by the mouth. These rascals deserve a punishment that no law now in existence can give them.

The Chinese make two kinds of pills (both of which contain opium) that are used by some smokers to assist them in breaking the habit. Finding the number of pills that will carry him through the day comfortably, the person at once abandons the pipe, taking the pills in its stead, reducing the number of pills from day to day, until none are taken. Some few have succeeded in thus curing themselves. Others dissolve the ash or *yen tshi* in sherry wine, and take a tablespoonful three times a day, each time adding to the bottle the same quantity of pure wine. Soon the patient is only taking clear wine and finds his habit broken.

CHAPTER VIII.

Opium-smoking amongst the Chinese—The responsibility of the English government—Rapid spread of the vice—Import statistics—
The two opium wars—Chinese laws against the practice—Effects
of the vice on the individual and the nation—Morality—Finance
—Pathology—How to remedy the evil.

THE picture of a nation with a population estimated at four hundred million, and whose
country covers an area equivalent to nearly one half
of all Europe,—one whose people are but slowly re-
sponding to missionary effort, forced, under protest
and at the point of the bayonet, by a Christian
nation to receive, almost duty free, a drug that is
ruining its people physically, mentally, morally, and
financially, that is emasculating its men, rendering
sterile its women, increasing its paupers and crimi-
nals, decimating and corrupting the ranks of its
statesmen, officials, and military, and stultifying all
efforts to advance the cause of the Christian religion,
is indeed saddening and pitiable.

This nation of Christians, deaf alike to protest
and appeal, maintaining their dictum by force of
arms in the face of facts from which a school-boy
could draw more just conclusions, when asked to

put an end to this digraceful and inhuman traffic, replies: "How can we do without the revenue? What would become of India?"

Better do without the revenue and India also, than to support it upon the financial and moral ruin of the Chinese. Must a nation of 400,000,000 be ruined here and hereafter, to give employment to and support the English rule over a nation of 200,-000,000? Does it not look ridiculous to see a nation fostering another nation's vice with a yearly profit to itself of $50,000,000, and at the same time endeavoring to convert the vicious to the Christian religion at a yearly expense of about half a million dollars? The account is far from balancing.

It has been urged by certain politicians that the culture of the poppy in India gives employment to a multitude of people that would otherwise be idle and poor. If these same people were *forced* to grow cereals as they now are *forced* to grow the poppy, if the same money was expended, the same care exercised in watching the rayots, the same trusty agents sent to consult the popular taste, a great evil would be done away with, and the growers be richer and happier than they are to-day. Moreover, the revenue would, in a measure, be maintained.

It has been said that those opposed to the opium trade are extremists, who delight to sound the alarm, and to upbraid a government, and do away with a revenue the evils resulting from which they either wilfully or unwittingly misrepresent. Is it so? Was the article in question some cereal, would the hare-brained extremists, so-called, attack the pro-opium party? No. Then it is the article itself to which objections are raised, and it is against the pandering to another people's vice, English-made, that is condemned. The revenue question must be put aside. In the words of Mr. Hugh Mason, M. P., of England, "That which is morally wrong can never be politically right."

It has been urged that "the Chinese will have and smoke opium at any cost, and that if we (the English) do not furnish it to them, others will. So why, through the gratification of a mere whim, should we lose this immense revenue?"

Late one night, not long since, while returning from the opium dens in Mott Street, and I beg leave to emphasize the word *den*, I saw a very respectably dressed man lying dead drunk in a tenement-house door-way in Baxter Street. It was evident that he did not belong there. He had on a diamond shirt-stud that sparkled in the light of the gas lamp, and a heavy gold chain hung across his vest. Several suspicious characters were loitering in the door-ways near by. I stirred him up in no gentle manner, found out where he lived, and put him on a horse-car going his way, thus saving him from being robbed. As I walked on I thought, this man's position is typical of that of China; my position like that of the English. I might have said to myself: "Here, this man is sure to be robbed. Why not take all he has and thus better myself, for if I don't, somebody else will." Poor logic, and yet such as is indulged in by the pro-opium people—only they have *been* robbing and ruining the Chinese for years, and feel that they might better take what is left, and carry abuse to actual murder, lest some one else should step in and do it for them. Stop the opium trade and *educate* the half-stupid, drunken Chinamen to a knowledge of their own danger, and then robbery will be impossible. If the nation or the man despoils himself or itself it is nobody's fault, save that of the individual or the nation, and the only means of correcting it is by educating the people up to a certain standard. My old and much respected preceptor, Dr. Willard Parker, used to illustrate the uselessness of prohibition (with reference to alcohol) without a proper education of the people, as follows:

Let us suppose that we have ten men and their families living upon an island that is cut off from all communication with other countries. Grain and grape are grown and ardent spirits are manufactured. All the men but one are addicted to the habitual use of alcohol. Business is manifestly failing, the houses are becoming dilapidated, children are not sent to school, and the inhabitants are uncleanly and untidy. Interference from the outside, *stringent* measures to uproot the evil of spirit-drinking, however well meant, would only result in failure. Let us suppose, however, that through the quiet, sensible reasoning, and, more especially, the example of A (the temperate one), B, a hard drinker, begins to realize that alcohol is at the root of his ills, and decides to abandon it, and does so. C follows in B's steps. Now, if A, B, and C were to meet, talk over the evil times, and decide to at once put a stop to the use of liquor by their neighbors, a failure would be sure to result. But if, by word and example, *seven* out of the ten were to reform, and *they* decide to stop the practice amongst the remaining three, success would undoubtedly attend their efforts.

If, after England ceases to send opium to China, the Chinese continue to raise the poppy in their six large provinces now under cultivation, the fault will be theirs, and the efforts of a comparatively few well-disposed people will be of no avail, and the only way to blot out the practice will be to so educate the majority of the people that they may see and fully appreciate its evil effects, and find wherein they are better off without it than with it. When the majority decide, the minority must abide by that decision.

How many Chinamen are there who smoke opium? It is impossible to say accurately, but it is claimed that there are certainly all of 15,000,000 in the country itself, and many more in the outlying provinces and dependencies.

That there are those who do not believe the evil

to be so wide-spread as represented by most writers
may be seen by the following:

THE NUMBER OF OPIUM-SMOKERS IN CHINA.

The *North-China Daily News* (Shanghai) of 28th July, says :

We have received from the Imperial Maritime Customs' Printing-
Office, a copy of a publication on " Opium,"—a compilation of reports on the subject drawn up by the Commissioners at the different
treaty-ports by order of the Inspector-General, who prefaces them
with the following remarks :

1.—*Opium in China : how many smokers does the foreign drug
supply ?*—The following pages contain the results of an inquiry insti-
tuted to answer this question.

2.—The Commissioners of Customs at a score of ports along the
coast and on the Yangtsze were instructed by circular to make inquiry in their respective districts and draw up replies to questions ap-
pended to the circular. That circular and the Commissioners' reports are given here in full, and in a separate table the answers to
the questions will be found brought together for greater convenience.
With these questions and answers to start from, an answer to the
question at the head of this introductory note can be easily worked
out.

3.—In round numbers, the annual importation of foreign opium
may be said to amount to 100,000 chests, or, allowing 100 catties to
each chest, 10,000,000 catties (the *catty* is the Chinese pound : one
catty is equal to *one pound and a third avoirdupois*). When boiled
down and converted into what is known as prepared opium, the raw
drug loses about 30 per cent. in weight ; accordingly, 10,000,000 catties of the unprepared drug imported reach the hands of retailers as,
say, 7,000,000 catties of prepared opium. The catty is divided into
16 *liang* (ounces), and the *liang* into tenths called *mace ;* in 7,000,000
catties there are, therefore, [7,000,000 x 16 x 10] 1,120,000,000 mace
of prepared opium for smokers.

4.—Before reaching the smoker, opium pays the Chinese Government import duty and *li-kin* taxes amounting to, say, 100 *taels*, and is then sold at, say, 800 taels of Chinese sycee or silver [3*l.*=Tls. 10] per 100 catties : thus the total quantity retailed, *i. e.*, *imported*, may be said to be paid for with 56,000,000 taels, or

$$\left\{ \frac{70,000 \times 800}{10} \times 3 \right\} 16,800,000l.,$$

and one mace of prepared opium is consequently worth, say

$$\left\{ \frac{16,800,000l., \text{ or } 4,032,000,000 \text{ pence}}{1,120,000,000} \right\},$$

about threepence-halfpenny (English).

5.—Divided by the number of days in the year, the quantity of prepared opium smoked daily may be said to be

$$\left\{ \frac{1,120,000,000}{365} \right\} 3,068,493 \text{ mace, and the value}$$

[3,068,493 x 3.60] 11,046,573*d.*, or 46,027*l.*

6.—Average smokers consume 3 mace of prepared opium and spend about 10¾*d.* daily. This quantity is the same as $\frac{6}{15}$ths of an ounce avoirdupois, and suffices for from 30 to 40 pipes, *i. e.*, whiffs, "draws," or inhalations. If we divide the total number of mace consumed daily by the total quantity each average smoker consumes daily, we find that there are in round numbers above 1,000,000 smokers

$$\left\{ \frac{3,068,493}{3} \right\} \text{ of foreign opium.}$$

7.—The population of China is spoken of as amounting to more than 400,000,000, and may fairly be pronounced to be something above 300,000,000. Estimating the population at 300,000,000 and opium-smokers at 1,000,000, and proceeding with the calculation, the result is that 3⅓ in every 1,000 smoke ; that is, that opium-smoking is practised by *one third of one per cent.* of the population.

8.—In addition to the foreign drug, there is also the native product. Reliable statistics cannot be obtained respecting the total quantity produced. Ichang, the port nearest Szechuan, the province which is generally believed to be the chief producer and chief consumer of native opium, estimates the total production of native opium at 25,000 chests annually ; while another port, Ningpo, far away on the coast, estimates it at 265,000 chests. Treating all such replies as merely so many guesses, there are, it is to be remarked, two statements which may be taken as facts in this connection : the one is that, as far as we know to-day, the native opium produced does not exceed the foreign import in quantity ; and the other, that native opium was known, produced, and used long before any Europeans began the sale of the foreign drug along the coast. Granting, then, that the native product equals the foreign import, and that 100,000 chests are produced annually, and granting also that this quantity, when prepared, provides 1,120,000,000 mace of prepared opium for the annual consumption of 1,000,000 additional smokers, the number of opium-smokers in China may be said to be in all 2,000,000, or *two thirds of one per cent.* of the population. The native product sells for one half of the price obtained for the foreign drug, and may be estimated to be paid for with, say, 8,400,000*l.* by 1,000,000 smokers, who spend about 5¼*d.* apiece daily. The total amount spent by China on this luxury, produced at home and imported from abroad, is thus, say, 25,000,000*l.* annually.

9.—Examined in this way the result arrived at is that 200,000 chests, or almost 12,000 tons [1,680 catties=one ton], of unprepared opium are consumed annually by 2,000,000 opium-smokers ; that these smokers expend 25,000,000*l.* on opium ; that this is an expenditure of, say, from 5*d.* to 11*d.* daily by individual smokers ; and that all the smokers amount to only two thirds of one per cent. of the population. If more than 3 mace apiece is consumed daily by smokers, then smokers are less numerous ; if less than 3 mace, then smokers are more numerous, and smoking individually less harmful. The truth is that many smoke more than 3 mace and many less, but from the statistical point of view it is safe to say that opium-smokers in China constitute simply two thirds of one per cent. of the population.

On the supposition even that the quantity of native opium produced is ten times that of the foreign opium imported, the total will not yet suffice for the consumption of even four per cent. of the population. Four per cent. is a small percentage, but in China it means twelve millions of people. It is hardly credible, however, that native opium is produced in such quantity ; but whatever the number of opium-smokers may really be—and allowing that many people smoke without injury—there must in any case be a percentage of smokers for whom the habit works nothing but evil.

10.—Chinese who have studied the opium question are opposed to a traffic which more or less harms smokers now numbering, say, over 2,000,000, and annually increasing ; at the same time they admit that opium provides a large revenue, that the expenditure for opium and liability to the incidence of opium taxation touch an infinitesimally small percentage of the population, and that neither the finances of the state, nor the wealth of its people, nor the growth of its population, can be specially damaged by a luxury which only draws from 5*d*. to 11*d*. apiece a day from the pockets of those who indulge in it, and which is indulged in by only *two thirds of one per cent.* of the population. They admit all this, but they do not find in either the revenue produced or the statistical demonstration of its percentage innocuousness any sufficient reason for welcoming the growth of the trade or for desisting from the attempt to check the consumption of opium.

NOTE BY EDITOR OF " FRIEND OF CHINA."—We regret that the volume of Reports, to which Mr. Inspector-General Hart has prefixed the above preface, has not yet reached us. In the meantime, notwithstanding his high authority, we hesitate to accept the above low estimate of the number of opium-smokers in China. Dr. Lockhart (see his " Medical Missionary," p. 386) estimated the number in 1854 as about 3,000,000. Sir Rutherford Alcock (see Report East Indian Finance, 1871, p. 275) supposed there were three or four millions of smokers. Both these gentlemen entered into careful calculations, but they differed from Mr. Hart in supposing the daily average individual consumption to be one mace instead of three. Applying their basis of calculation to Mr. Hart's figures, we obtain 6,000,000 of smokers instead of two. This figure would have to be increased considerably by taking into account that a great part of the opium is smoked twice over. The ashes from the pipe are carefully collected and help to supply the craving of numerous poor votaries of the drug. Even so, the largest of these calculations does not come up to the opinion common among the Chinese themselves, that fully one half of the men indulge in the vice. Probably the natives reason from the condition of things in great cities like Foochow, Soochow, Peking, etc., and overlook the country populations, which are less tainted with the vice. The *North-China Daily News* in a leading article boldly characterizes Mr. Hart's statements as "wild," and enters into an elaborate argument to prove that " a majority of the adult male population of China smoke opium." Without at present going farther into this perplexing subject, one thing remains certain, and even Mr. Hart does not conceal it : *There is a deeply rooted conviction in the Chinese mind that opium does unutterable harm to the country.* No reasoning from statistics can touch this fact. If you prove that the smokers are few comparatively, then of the few smokers a large proportion must be visibly ruined, or this conviction could not have grown up and become universal. It is impossible to hold at once that the smokers are few and the evil results to them small. The fewer they are the more palpably destructive must the vice be, or Chinamen would never have come to regard the drug as an unmitigated curse to their land.

The first mention that we find made of the poppy by the Chinese is in their Herbal, written over 200 hundred years ago, in which the manner of raising the plant and collecting the juice are accurately described.[1] It is there known as *apien*. Both Williams and Shuck incline strongly to the belief that it was an " important article of commerce in the East long before Europeans had any

[1] Williams : The Middle Kingdom, etc., p. 382, Vol. 2.

direct intercourse with India." Previous to the
year 1767 the importation of opium into China
stood at about 200 chests per annum (Shuck). An
English writer[1] says, however, that at this date the
Portuguese were carrying to China about 1,000
chests annually.

In 1773 the English made their first venture (suggested by the fertile mind of the not over-scrupulous
Warren Hastings), which was not altogether a success. In 1799, so rapidly had the trade increased
and the vice spread, that the Emperor K'ien Lung
prohibited its import, without, however, in any way
limiting the amount entering the country, it, on the
contrary, rapidly increased through smuggling and
bribery. Commissioner Lin, in 1839, seized and
held Captain Elliot and the foreign merchants until
all opium then in port or on shipboard was surrendered to him. The 20,291 chests thus obtained
were destroyed. These were valued at about ten
million dollars. War was declared by England, in
1840, she claiming direct injury and insult, and
active measures were commenced in 1841. The
Chinese, fighting for their rights, were completely
subdued, and required to pay a war indemnity in
addition to the value of the opium destroyed.
Smuggling was continued without any stop and
with the full knowledge of the British government,

---

[1] The Facts of the Opium Trade, pamphlet, London, 1880.

the Chinese law remaining the same, until 1860, when, after another war, the Chinese were pitilessly forced to legalize the trade, and admit the death-dealing drug under a small duty. An appeal in 1869, remarkable for its logic, humane expression, and a realization of the danger that was threatening her people, was made by the Chinese to the English government, who disdainfully passed it by un-noticed. An agreement made by representatives of the English government with the Chinese to raise the tariff one half, was also repudiated by the home government, and to-day England is in the unpleas-ant position of direct responsibility for having fostered and forced a vice that numbers fifteen millions among its victims,—a position for which the only justification offered was the statement that the Indian Empire needed the blood-money thus obtained. The Chinese *smokers* themselves are not free from blame, but every honest observer *must* believe that if China had been allowed to have her own way the vice, to-day, would be nearly dead. The total defeat of the Chinese government by the English, the one fighting against the other for the introduction of the besotting drug, acted badly upon the smokers, for when they saw their own government worsted in such a contest, they took heart and found spirit to defy the laws of their country.

Has the practice really spread with the rapidity that is claimed? In 1773, the amount entering China stood at 1,000 chests as against 200 chests the year before. Calkins gives the following figures as representing the importations from India into China:

1767 = 200 caissons.
1800–1810 = 2,500 piculs = 337,500 pounds.
1820 = 4,700 (7,000 ?) piculs = 627,450 pounds (934,500 lbs.?).
1830 = 18,700 " = 2,496,450 "
1840 = 50,000 " = 6,675,000 "
1850 = 55,000 " = 7,342,500 "
1860 = 60,000 (estimated) " = 8,010,000 "
1867 = 75,000 " = 10,012,500 "

" For the later (since 1867) decennial periods," says Calkins, " there has been a falling off below the two per cent. of annual increase that was a reduction variously ascribed to poverty, increasing celibacy, and impaired fecundity and infanticide,— the direct and palpable offshoots of the national vice."

He says, further, that we may fairly estimate the home production as 25 per cent. of the importations, and the contraband traffic at 12½ per cent.

The following figures are taken from the U. S. Consular Reports for the years 1874–5–6–7, and represent the amount of opium entering China for these years:

KIND.	POUNDS.*	VALUE.*	YEAR.
Malwa	5,834,796,039	$27,628,993.98	
Patna	757,851,345	9,522,851.10	
Benares	268,180,069	4,379,070.67	
Other kinds	35,299,565	454,313.79	1874
	6,896,127,018	$41,985,229.54	
Malwa	5,165,911,995	$23,601,286.59	
Patna	2,058,557,985	8,860,097.60	
Benares	1,004,026,080	4,130,592.02	
Other kinds	57,092,885	681,965.34	1875
	8,285,588,945	$37,273,941.55	
Malwa	5,866,850,165	$26,498,242.05	
Patna	2,138,615,265	9,207,962.40	
Benares	1,150,;93,655	4,721,914.89	
Other kinds	174,129,390	759,801.84	1876
	9,330,088,475	$41,187,921.18	
Malwa	5,571,221.32	$28,153,936.86	
Patna	2,035,573.29	9,032,621.74	
Benares	1,444,696.95	6,002,340.75	
Other kinds	322,415.18	1,313,256.84	1877
	9,373,905.75	$44,502,156.19	

There is some question in my mind about the correctness of these figures, for the following, apparently authentic, are at variance with them.

The subjoined figures are given for the year 1875. The Indian Returns of Trade published in this country since 1875 are abbreviated, and therefore we cannot bring the figures of later dates. But the general character of the trade is unaltered :—

* Reduced from piculs (133½ lbs.) and from taels ($1.47).

Exports from India to China (including Hong Kong) in 1875.[1]

Raw Cottons	.	.	.	.	.	.	. value	£439,470
Piece Goods and Sundries	.	.	.	.	.	"	346,025
Opium	.	.	.	.	.	.	.	"	10,862,694

£11,648,189

Imports from China (including Hong Kong) into India in 1875.

Raw Silk	.	.	.	.	.	.	.	value	£691,569
Manufactured Silk	.	.	.	.	.	"	253,108
Tea	.	.	.	.	.	.	.	.	"	120,960
Sundries	.	.	.	.	.	.	.	"	454,477

£1,520,114

This shows a balance due from China to India of more than ten millions sterling, nearly the whole being for opium. China paid in gold and silver £1,334,274,[2] leaving a balance due of over eight millions and a half. The average balance against China for the previous five years was £8,372,398.[3] *

By 1867, the amount imported had reached the enormous quantity of 81,750 chests.

Of this 37,775 chests were from Malwa and valued at	$30,510,867
43,975 " " Patna and Benares "	27,717,442
Giving as a total	$58,228,309

paid by the Chinese for opium—opium that does not leave there for any other port, and that is wholly consumed in smoking. In 1867 the total value of

---

[1] Statement of the Trade of British India with British Possessions and Foreign Countries, for the five years 1870–71 to 1874–75. [C.—1616, pp. 216—219.]

[2] *Ibid.*, pp. 15, 16.   [3] *Ibid.*, p. xxxii.

* Fourth Annual Report of the Anglo-Oriental Society for the Suppression of the Opium Trade, London, 1880.

the opium imported was 45,000,000 taels, or about $63,000,000.[1]

The enormous amount consumed yearly may be better understood from the following figures:

37,775 chests of Malwa opium, at 136 lbs. to the chest, = ...	5,137,300	pounds
43,975 chests of Patna, etc., opium, at 116 lbs. to the chest, = ...	5,101,100	"
	10,238,400	"

This would make OVER 500 TONS of opium consumed in China, in 1867, not counting the amount produced at home and the quantity smuggled and coming from other nations, which would bring it close to 700 TONS.

Calkins, whom I have so often quoted, says a little farther on:

Compare now, by way of contrast, 1867 with 1840. To the 50,000 pounds of 1840 add 25 per cent. (for the home culture) making no allowance for clandestine importations when there was little or no inducement to such,[2] the ratio of advance for the 27 years is as 185:100, which, compounded with that of population, gives an overplus of 66.5 per cent., viz., an increase upon 1840 of 5 to 3.

In 1840 the East India Company realized out of the opium traffic with China the sum of $4,000,000; in 1850 the receipts reached $15,000,000, a figure which had doubled by 1858. More than ten years back (1854) the Chinese paid this company for opium alone a sum exceeding in valuation the total export of their teas and silks to-

---

[1] China Overland Trade Reports, quoted by Speer, "China and the United States."

[2] There being no duty imposed at that time. —K.

gether.   Indeed, as Dr. Allen [1] has calculated, the annual surplus
profit, at the time, for this branch of trade alone, was adequate to
the liquidation, in the course of seven years, of the twenty million
debt that had been incurred by the act of colonial emancipation,
principal and interest both:

  To such proportions has this species of trade, tentatively undertaken
by a few roving mariners now calumniated, fostered as it has been by
the indomitable greed of English merchantmen.   The humanizing
tendencies of British civilization, as enforced and supported by British
artillery, are very palpably illustrated in a saying current among the
people of China, of this sort : '' During the opium war the English
gave their Chinese acquaintance cannon balls of iron, and after the
war cannon balls of opium ; [2] so that our people had the desperate
privilege of choice as between being shot to death and poisoned to
death.''

  What a tremendous money drain this is upon the
Chinese Empire ! She really gives all the tea she
can raise, the country's most important industry, to
purchase a drug that panders to a vice. How many
million tea-growers slave their lives out to pay for
the beastiality of their countrymen !

  Furthermore, recent consular reports assure us
that the amount of opium entering China from
Persia has enormously increased since 1873.   At
that date the import stood at 558 piculs, 74,493
pounds, while in 1879 it reached 5,300 piculs, or
731,400 pounds.

  The following statistics, taken from " Our National Responsibility for the Opium Trade,'' [3] are of value.

---

[1] The Opium Trade, N. Allen, M.D., Lowell, 1853.
[2] As packed in the cases the balls of opium are not unlike cannon balls.—K.
[3] Published by English Anti-Opium Society.

Number of Chests of Bengal and Malwa Opium exported to China and places beyond British India. Compiled from Finance and Revenue Accounts, published in Calcutta, by Government, in 1875. Part III, Accounts No. 65 and No. 67.

Official Year.	From Bengal.			Price realized at Government sale, per chest.	Malwa opium exported from Bombay to China.	Total export.
	To China.	Singapore, Penang, etc.	Total.			
	Chests.	Chests.	Chests.	£	Chests.	Chests.
1830–31	5,590	1,526	7,116	176	4,610	11,726
1831–32	6,750	757	7,507	158	10,679	18,186
1832–33	7,540	1,845	9,385	124	6,698	16,083
1833–34	10,151	1,779	11,930	101	10,855	22,785
1834–35	9,480	1,570	11,050	111	6,812	17,862
1835–36	13,021	1,786	14,807	127	—	—
1836–37	10,493	2,241	12,734	155	20,882½	33,616½
1837–38	16,112	3,195	19,307	87	10,372½	29,679½
1838–39	14,499	3,722	18,221	53	17,353	35,574
1839–40	3,755	14,755	18,510	42	—	—
1840–41	5,817	11,593	17,410	70	12,022½	29,432½
1841–42	10,752	8,987	19,739	75	14,473	34,212
1842–43	11,867	4,651	16,518	112	19,369	35,887
1843–44	13,067	4,792	17,859	132	16,944	34,803
1844–45	14,709	4,083	18,792	132	18,150½	36,942½
1845–46	16,265	4,288	20,553	136	17,770	38,323
1046–47	20,668	4,322	24,990	123	17,389½	42,379½
1847–48	19,434	4,443	23,877	98	19,391	43,268
1848–49	27,870	4,417	32,287	90	21,392¼	53,679¼
1849–30	30,996	4,097	35,093	102	16,513	51,606
1850–51	28,892	4,010	32,902	95	19,138	52,040
1851–52	27,921	4,385	32,306	98	28,168½	60,474½
1852–33	31,433	4,745	36,178	110	24,979½	61,157½
1853–54	33,941	6,854	40,795	88	26,113½	66,908½
1854–55	43,952	7,469	51,421	71	25,958¼	77,379¼
1855–56	37,851	7,087	44,938	83	25,576	70,514
1856–57	36,459	5,982	42,441	89	29,846½	72,287½
1857–58	31,878	6,735	38,613	128	36,125½	74,738½
1858–59	33,858	827	34,685	148	40,849	75,534
1859–60	22,329	3,621	25,950	167	32,534	58,484
1860–61	15,688	3,621	19,309	192	43,691	63,000
1861–62	21,332	5,240	26,572	161	38,680	65,252
1862–63	25,846	6,815	32,661	142	49,485½	82,146½
1863–64	33,815	8,806	42,621	121	28,210½	70,831½
1864–65	41,719	8,484	50,203	93	34,213½	84,416½
1865–66	42,697	11,576	54,273	112	34,166½	88,439½
1866–67	37,279	4,478	41,757	124	33,081	74,838
1867–68	40,772	7,484	48,256	133	38,883	87,139
1868–69	37,985	6,281	44,266	137	30,683	74,949
1869–70	43,054	6,680	49,734	119	38,694	88,428
1870–71	40,669	8,054	48,723	112	36,436	85,159
1871–72	41,569	7,886	49,455	138	39,334½	88,789½
1872–73	34,009	6,476	40,485	138	42,369	82,854
1873–74	34,820	8,517	43,337	126	45,301	88,638
*1874–75	—	—	45,000	120	49,212	94,212
1875–76	—	—	45,510	125	42,490½	88,000½
1876–77	—	—	47,240	127	49,136	96,376
1877–78	—	—	49,500	126	45,830	95,330

* From 1874 the figures are taken from the Blue-Books published in London, East India Finance and Revenue Accounts.

Net Opium Revenue (distinguishing Receipts from the Monopoly and from Duty on Malwa Opium), compared with the Total Net Revenue of India, from 1834-35. From the Calcutta Blue-Book, Finance and Revenue Accounts, 1875. Part III. Accounts No. 2 and No. 64.

	Net Opium Revenue.			Total Net Revenue of India.
Years.	Bengal.	Bombay.	Total.	
	£	£	£	£
1834-35	694,279	144,171	838,450	14,392,309
1835-36	1,320,162	171,845	1,492,007	14,336,985
1836-37	1,334,097	200,871	1,534,968	16,116,431
1837-38	1,436,724	149,721	1,586,445	15,953,783
1838-39	698,799	254,331	953,130	16,425,885
1839-40	326,076	11,701	337,777	15,530,757
1840-41	649,632	224,645	874,277	16,323,563
1841-42	803,867	214,899	1,018,766	17,190,613
1842-43	1,322,343	251,238	1,576,581	17,933,635
1843-44	1,675,948	348,878	2,024,826	18,593,560
1844-45	1,808,345	372,943	2,181,288	18,685,119
1845-46	2,207,726	595,624	2,803,350	19,319,036
1846-47	2,279,339	606,863	2,886,202	20,071,289
1947-48	1,291,529	371,855	1,663,384	19,369,432
1848-49	1,958,256	887,507	2,845,763	20,082,202
1849-50	2,800,797	729,484	3,530,281	22,202,898
1850-51	2,055,827	694,521	2,750,348	21,374,223
1851-52	2,011,163	1,128,083	3,139,246	21,693,687
1852-53	2,601,043	1,116,889	3,717,932	23,374,748
1853-54	2,394,998	649,022	3,359,020	22,691,319
1854-55	2,232,411	1,101,191	3,333,602	23,529,289
1855-56	2,951,612	1,010,365	3,961,977	25,375,580
1856-57	2,700,712	1,159,677	3,860,389	26,305,111
1857-58	4,286,377	1,631,998	5,918,375	25,285,958
1858-59	3,898,114	1,448,277	5,346,391	28,759,597
1859-60	3,636,453	1,533,325	5,169,778	31,318,097
1860-61	3,316,613	2,441,679	5,758,292	34,198,019
1861-62	2,471,347	2,438,458	4,909,805	34,486,759
1862-63	2,959,789	3,239,409	6,199,198	35,926,232
1863-64	3,044,688	1,480,818	4,525,506	34,447,543
1864-65	2,883,542	2,100,882	4,984,424	35,306,234
1865-66	4,499,227	2,124,767	6,623,994	36,816,787
1866-67	3,873,754	1,851,263	5,725,017	33,434,179
1867-68	4,695,357	2,352,708	7,048,065	37,274,048
1868-69	4,927,150	1,804,180	6,731,330	36,701,536
1869-70	3,776,626	2,354,246	6,130,872	37,862,424
1870-71	3,632,325	2,398,709	6,031,034	38,719,877
1871-72	5,305,402	2,351,811	7,657,213	39,076,952
1872-73	4,259,162	2,611,261	6,870,423	38,946,763
*1873-74	3,584,763	2,738,836	6,323,599	40,442,903
1874-75	3,264,266	2,950,817	6,215,083	41,059,405
1875-76	3,705,170	2,547,690	6,252,860	41,826,784
1876-77	3,334,338	2,946,475	6,280,813	39,168,627
1877-78	3,773,960	2,747,496	6,521,456	38,656,484

NOTE.—According to a return printed 2d May, 1879, the net opium revenue for 1878-79 is estimated at £7,584,062, and the total net revenue at £44,554,375.
* From 1873-74 the figures are taken from the East India Finance and Revenue Accounts, published in London.

Total Quantity of Opium imported into China during the years 1864-72. Compiled from published Returns of the Chinese Imperial Maritime Customs.

Description.		Quantity.		Value.
		Piculs.[1]	Catties.	Haikwan Taels.[2]
Malwa	India	295,730	97	127,164,317
Patna		141,662	52	56,665,008
Benares		75,374	24	30,149,696
Persian		9,204	23	3,773,734
Turkey		235	95	89,661
Total		522,207	291	217,842,416

The above table shows conclusively that the opium trade is a question between China and Great Britain alone; the other countries interested in the trade, Turkey and Persia, are interested only to a very small extent. Out of a total import of more than half a million piculs in nine years, these countries together sent only 9,440 piculs,—not one fiftieth of the whole.

[1] The Picul = 100 catties = 133⅓ lbs. avoirdupois.

[2] The Haikwan Tael = 6s. 8d.

We have not the figures to complete the above tables to the present date, but the following extract from the Chinese Imperial Maritime Customs for 1878 shows that the proportions of the trade are still about the same.

IMPORT OF OPIUM INTO CHINA.

Description.	1877.		1878.	
	Quantity.	Value.	Quantity.	Value.
	Piculs.	Taels.	Piculs.	Taels.
Malwa . . .	41,705	19,141,281	37,004	19,301,062
Patna . . .	15,237	6,139,994	18,588	6,948,522
Benares . . .	10,821	4,083,225	12,373	4,406,269
Other kinds . .	2,415	893,372	4,458	1,607,104
Total . .	70,178	30,257,812	72,423	32,262,957

Effects upon the Morals.—What are the effects of this practice upon the morals? In the first place, we have the united testimony of the missionaries of all faiths and from all nations, that the opium trade, and the vice of opium-smoking, are the greatest barriers to the spread of the true belief amongst these people. They, not illogically, fail to see how the religion of a country that has, up to the present time, forced a vice upon them through two wars, can be any better than their own. They cannot understand the principle that actuates a so-called Christian nation to spread the Gospel through the agency of a few hundred poorly-paid missionaries, and which avenges a fanciful slight, and insists upon the moral, mental, and physical injury of the whole nation by armed thousands and at a cost of millions. It is not surprising that they cannot understand that which is still a mystery to those who are better able to judge.

The use of opium being regarded by the Chinese as a vice, no opium-smoker can be received into the Christian Church. The heathen perpetually bring this opium trade as a reproach to the Christian missionary. In 1869 Bishop Schereschewsky, of the American Episcopal Church, was driven out of Kaifengfu, the capital of Honan Province, by a mob which followed him, shouting, "You burned our palace, you killed our emperor, you *sell poison* to the people, and now you come to teach us virtue !" In 1877 a number of Chinese gentlemen, formed into an association for the promotion of abstinence from opium, published an appeal to our countrymen containing this home thrust : " The New Testament says, ' Whatsoever ye would that men should do unto you, do ye even so unto them.' Is it possible that the instruction of the Saviour has never yet reached the ears of your honored country ? " [1]

[1] The Facts of the Opium Trade, London, 1880.

Upon the morals of the individual the effects are well marked. The continued smoking of this drug plunges the victim into a state of lethargy that knows no higher sentiment, hope, ambition, or longing than the gratification of this diseased appetite. It blunts all the finer sensibilities, and cases the individual in a suit of vicious armor, that is as little likely to be pierced by the light of true morality as a rhinoceros hide by a willow twig. To him, Heaven is equivalent to plenty of the drug, Hell, to abstinence from it.

Once fastened upon the victim, the craving knows no amelioration; it is a steady growth with each succeeding indulgence, gaining strength as the huge snow-ball gains in circumference and weight by its onward movement. No wonder that laws have failed to blot it out. A man may wish to be free from it, as may a dove in the talons of an eagle, or a lamb in the embrace of a tiger, and with as little good result. The awakening comes too late.

In Hoopih, the experiment of cutting away a portion of the upper lip, so as to prevent the smoker from using the pipe, was tried and failed.[1]

Mr. Lord, United States consul to Ningpo, whose long residence in China entitles his opinion to the highest consideration, says : "The demand for opium, when the demand exists, is imperative.

---

[1] Chinese Repository, vol. viii, No. 7.

Opium-smokers must have opium and in most cases they must have
it in increasing quantities. To obtain it, no obstacle is too great to
be overcome. They will part with everything for it ; sacrifice everything that is sacred. The wretch who is given to opium is lost to
everything else. His land, his house, his bed, his clothes, his food,
his wife, his children, and even his life, will all be consumed on the
altar of this terrible Moloch. Of course, a trade resting upon such
support, can defy all obstacles, and live even in the midst of floods
and famines." [1]

Twenty-five years ago Surgeon Smith observed in Pulo Penang that
penal enactments had failed to stem the tide, and that thefts, robber-
ies, and murders, too, were being perpetrated again and again, and
increasingly in numbers, so impetuous and uncontrollable does this
perverted appetite for opium fumes become. [2]

Severe punishment, even decapitation, has been
promised to all concerned in the trade and the use, [3]
but with no result.

Consul Smithers, of Chi-Kiang, China, writes : [4]

The consumption of foreign opium by all classes is shown to be
annually increasing, and the native production, although against the
law, is not inconsiderable. In 1877 the British Government sent a
mission to Yunnan, in Central China, composed of three intelligent
gentlemen, who were instructed to report on the geographical, commercial, and political character of the country. From Mr. Daven-
port's report the following is taken : "Opium was growing all along
the route from the entry into Sezechuen until we arrived in Momieu,
while in Yunnan it was to be seen not only outside but inside the
city walls, yet its cultivation is strictly prohibited by the penal code.

[1] Extract from Secretary Evarts' Report, for 1879, on Commercial Relations
to the House of Representatives of the United States.
[2] Calkins, *op. cit.*, p. 369.
[3] Portfolio Chinensis, Macao, 1840.
[4] U. S. Consular Reports, No. 9, July, 1881.

In an edition published in Peking by the government, in 1871, of foreigners who bring opium into China, the principals are punishable with decapitation, and their accessories with immediate strangulation. Native growers and those who manufacture opium, if it amounts to 500 liang (about 30 lbs. avoirdupois), are sentenced to strangulation, the carrying out of the sentence to be deferred, and the accessories to military servitude for life at distant and pestilential frontiers ; the landlords having a guilty knowledge to military servitude at distant frontiers and confiscation of the misused land, while the neighbors and constables have to undergo 100 blows each from heavy bambs for not reporting the offence to the authorities. Mandarins convicted of smoking are forever deprived of their position in the service and banished to Tartary, while the unhappy eunuch caught smoking within the precincts of the palace is sentenced to wear the congue (a wooden collar weighing 33½ pounds) for the rest of his natural life at the most distant and pestilential frontiers under the custody of the local officers, not being pardoned even when a general act of grace has been issued by the emperor."

How firmly rooted must this habit be to dare so much for the purpose of gratifying its cravings! Shuck [1] speaks in the same strain :

Upon its use and abuse as a luxury no observation is offered at present, further than to record the most unqualified disapproval of both. For the sake of regaling themselves with opium, all classes of the Chinese will face every hazard to obtain it, violating the laws of the land, braving the official prohibitions, and risking their own lives and the lives of their families. Some of the high officers, too, have been wont to issue flaming proclamations against its importation and use, while at the same time they themselves have been regarded and placarded as notorious opium-smugglers and opium-smokers.

---

[1] Portfolio Chinensis, p. 13.

Indeed, the late Emperor, Taou Kwang, is said by Tiedeman[1] to have himself been a victim to the habit, breaking himself of it, however, warned by failing health that it was doing him injury. I can hardly believe, however, that the man who said, when asked to legalize the traffic in opium, " No, nothing shall induce me to derive revenue from the vice and misery of my own people," could have been an opium-smoker. Surgeon Smith, of Pulo-Penang,[2] however, also says that the fact was widely and well known.

Nor do these extracts as to the loss of moral tone by the opium-smoker stand alone. There is an abundance of testimony upon this point ; not mere heresay evidence, but actual facts.

Another thing, which, by the way, is portrayed in the series of Chinese plates known as "The Opium-Smoker," is that for the first few months the sexual appetite is markedly increased, and the habitué finds pleasure in the companionship of dissolute men and lewd women. Instead of a normal sexual tone, the appetite is exalted to a veritable condition of satyriasis in the male and nymphomania in the female. This increase of sexual appetite is most marked in women Indeed, the laws against opium-smoking that have been enacted and enforced in this country had their inception in a knowledge of the fact that

[1] Quoted by Calkins, *op. cit.*, p. 200.   [2] Chinese Repository, Nov., 1842.

male smokers (Americans), understanding this matter, were continually beguiling women and young
girls to try the pipe, and effected their ruin when
they were under its influence.

After a time even normal desire and power are ob-
tunded or totally destroyed.

THE OPIUM PIPE AS A PAUPERIZING AGENT.

Financially, the ill effects of this practice are quite
as well marked.   There are three factors here working to a common end, *i. e.*, (*a*) the necessity of paying out money for a costly drug, (*b*) the loss of
money through inattention to business, and (*c*) the
loss of interest in family, children, and friends, as
also of self-respect,—the great incentives to work.
So far as moral deterioration and financial ruin are
concerned I should unhesitatingly head the list with
the habitual use of the opium pipe.   In the old prov-
erb " Procrastination is the thief of time," the term
opium-pipe might, with justice, be substituted for
procrastination.   The injecter of morphia or the
taker of opium inserts his dose or swallows his
bolus and there the matter ends, but the opium-
smoker spends hours in the tedious cooking and
preparing of the *tschandu* for the bowl.   Much of
the charm of opium-smoking, so the confirmed
habitués tell me, lies in this very laziness and slow-
ness of movement.   To them the process is not

tedious, and with pleasant companionship the hours are gone before they are aware of it. Thus the smoker will dawdle through a whole day, wasting the hours, that, if devoted to honest effort, would bring money to his pocket and happiness to his family. In this country even the lowest class of white smokers, the petty thieves, gamblers, and the like, recognize this wanton waste of time, and commonly remark, "The pipe has 'differed' me a thousand times," that is to say, has caused them to lose opportunities by which they might have profited; a good thing, so far as their evil deeds are concerned, but a very poor agent with which to reform them.

Calkins states that:

Hong-merchants, who have come to naught in their commercial transactions, are found generally to have broken down on the chandoo, etc.

[1] The poor smoker who has pawned every article in his possession, still remains idle; and when the periodical thirst comes on will even pawn his wives and sell his daughters. In the province of Ngauwhui I once saw a man named Chin, who, being childless, purchased a concubine and got her with child; afterwards, when his money was expended and other means all failed him, being unable to resist the desire for the pipe, he sold her, in her pregnancy, for several tens of dollars. This money being expended he went and hung himself. Alas, how painful was his end!

Williams says:

[2] The evils suffered and the crimes committed by the desperate

---

[1] Chinese Repository, vol. 7, p. 181.
[2] The Middle Kingdom, vol. 2, p. 394.

victims of the opium-pipe are dreadful and multiplied. Theft, arson, murder, and suicide are perpetrated in order to obtain it or escape its effects.

If the physical ill wrought by opium-smoking is less than that resulting from the other modes of using the drug, the moral deterioration is much greater. Calkins says :

1. The *moral aspect* presented by the opium-eater is that in which the negative qualities, rather, are what stand out in relief. The will-power being now prostrate, though indeed self-consciousness has survived, the mind appears sunk in a somnolent and impassive quiescence. Under this spiritual thraldom all the generous sympathies shrink within themselves and fade, the relish for society and its enjoyments is extinguished, and the abject sufferer courses along "spe pendulus horæ," buffeted by wind and wave, without power to shape his course, without resolution to make the effort, drifting toward a lurid and desolate shore, to be thenceforward cut off from the living world as by a Styx nine times intervening.

This phase of moral obtuseness Huc adverts to thus : " The spectacle of the family brought to extreme distress, the cries of wife and children, extorted by the pangs of hunger and the pinchings of cold, fail to revive in the parent so much perhaps as a momentary recognition. Such stolidity under abasement is less an index of callous indifference than an implied conviction of helplessness and a settled gloom too deep for Hope's cheering ray to pierce,—

For a mortal coldness o'er the soul like a death-damp has stole on ;
It cannot feel for others' woes, it dare not dream its own.' "

" The days of the opium-eater (as observes the Hon. Mr. Tiffany, of the India service) pass along, divided between sloth and remorse, and when night with its pall shuts in the day, again he falls, palsied and unresisting, into the trail of the sorceress that mocks with her finger as she beckons him on."

And again :

Assam, as appears from the account by Bruce, presents an equally ugly picture. " Opium is the plague-spot that threatens to depopulate this beautiful country. Here is a people, once vigorous and thriving, now the most demoralized and degenerate of all the tribes of India. As in China, where population has fallen off from an annual advance of three per cent. to one-third this, so here the natural increase is visibly kept down through impaired fecundity ; and as for old men there are very few indeed. Deplorable as is the physical corruption of the Assamese, their moral debasement is even worse. Eking out existence in a miserable effeminacy, and utterly impervious to any sense of shame, they will recklessly go to any excess for the procuring of their stimulus, even to the bartering of wife and children."

Another very decided factor, both in working moral deterioration and spreading the vice, is the fact of the companionship, two usually smoking together. In this country many honest and respectable young men and women have been led to try the pipe, and, forming the habit, have continued its use, and been corrupted by association with low companions, who led them so far as even to commit crimes. One pertinent instance is where a young telegraph operator was, after a time, persuaded by a party of sporting men, whom he daily met in the " den," to tamper with the telegraph wires, so as to make false returns regarding a certain race. As it did no harm beyond defrauding some pool-room sharpers nothing is to be regretted, but it shows to what purposes the companionship may lead. Had this man never smoked he would never have met these people, and they would not have dared to approach him upon the subject.

The evil effects of this companionship was recognized and dwelt on by the King of Siam in his edict,[1] and is spoken of also by many Chinese writers. In Siam the vice has attained enormous proportions. I, myself, know of instances where Americans have degenerated into veritable opium fiends, smoking almost constantly, and, sacrificing everybody and everything to their gluttinous appetite for the drug. One case in particular suggests itself to my mind: R., a Scotchman about thirty years of age, of good family and good education. He began the practice some ten years ago while in San Francisco, and save for a short interval of abstinence some four years ago has been a very hard smoker. Through it he lost his engagement as an opera-singer, could be found day after day in a low den in Mott street smoking the vilest opium to be had, greedily scraping the bowl and eating the ash or *yen tshi*, leaving his wife and baby, then fallen to a single room in a Baxter Street tenement house, to starve while he stolidly and indifferently worshipped his idol. He would lie, would beg and borrow from his friends until they avoided him, would, in fact, re-

---

[1] Singapore *Free Press*, June 13, 1839. Sir John Browning, The Kingdom and People of Siam, London, 1857.

sort to any means to get opium. His appetite for food was gone, his sleep broken by horrible dreams, his clothing saturated by the opium-stained perspiration, his person filthy, his dress slovenly and his bowels constipated. His voice was wrecked and his ambition wholly drowned in the sea of opium fumes. When I saw him he had lost about seventy pounds in weight.

I took him into my Home, and in a short time had freed him of his habit. The change in his appearance was marvelous. The skin became clear, the eyes bright, a look of blank stupidity was exchanged for one of intelligence, hope appeared, care for his family returned with renewed force, ambition resumed its sway, and he was himself again. In eleven days he gained sixteen pounds in weight, and up to the present time—some three months—has gone on steadily improving.

The financial question as affecting the Chinese nation has already been spoken of.

PATHOLOGICAL EFFECT OF OPIUM-SMOKING.

Upon the subject of the pathological effects of opium-smoking upon the individual and the nation, I must insist that there has been a great deal of unintentional misunderstanding and exaggeration. I base what I have to say, not upon hearsay or conjecture, but upon careful study of American and

Chinese smokers, both during the period of use and of total abstinence. What I am about to say I can demonstrate to any one from cases now under my care, and from the full histories of cases that I have treated. Having, for the past few years been engaged almost exclusively in the treatment of all forms of the opium-habit, I must claim that my opportunities have placed me in an exceptionally favorable position to judge of the comparative evils wrought by the different manners of using the drug.

One very grave mistake that has been made by many of the anti-opium trade writers and speakers has been, to judge of the ill effects of the habitual use of the opium-pipe by the ill effects that have been found to result from the use of the drug by the mouth or hypodermically.

Thus, the effects of opium-taking amongst the natives of Burmah, the description of which is unquestionably truthful,[1] cannot be taken as a fair gauge by which to judge of the effect upon the Chinese, for, while the former swallow it,[2] the latter smoke it.

The Evil Effects of Its Use Upon a Weak Race.—The use or abuse of opium has done so much harm in Burmah that the authorities find themselves compelled to place new restrictions on its consumption. Whatever could be done to lessen the consumption by artificially increasing the price has been done. There are very heavy import duties on opium and still heavier duties on the sale in the shape of taxes for licenses to keep opium-houses. In one way or another the selling price in Burmah is ten times what the drug costs when it reaches a Burmese port. It was thought that by thus enhancing the cost the general consumption of opium would be checked, while there would be

[1] Annual Report of the Society for the Suppression of the Opium Trade, 1881.

[2] Some Burmese unquestionably smoke, but the majority swallow the bolus.

enough to meet what is termed in the report of the Chief Commissioner a *bona fide* demand, and that the revenue would gain all that could be gained for it without provoking a system of illegitimate supply. But in one respect these expectations have been signally disappointed. The revenue has largely profited, and the *bona fide* demand has been amply provided for, but the general consumption has not been checked. On the contrary, the consumption in 1879 was double what it was in 1869, and the consequences have been most lamentable. To the Burmese, opium was a novelty, and it had all the attractions of a novelty and of a thing which it was at once pleasant and wrong to enjoy. A race physically weak, having no personal or hereditary power of bearing the ill effects of opium, ignorant of the consequences of indulgence, or reckless of those consequences when placed beyond doubt, was sure to exhibit in the shortest possible time all the worst evils that excessive use of opium can engender. Among the Burmese, it is officially stated, the habitual use of the drug saps the physical and mental energies, destroys the nerves, emaciates the body, predisposes to disease, induces indolent and filthy habits of life, destroys self-respect, is one of the most fertile sources of misery, destitution, and crime, fills the jails with men of relaxed frame, predisposed to dysentery and cholera, prevents the due extension of cultivation and the development of the land revenue, checks the natural gowth of the population, and enfeebles the constitution of succeeding generations.—*London Saturday Review.*

In the matter of physical injury, both as regards rapidity of action and permanency of effect, the different preparations of the drug and the manner of using them may be arranged in the following order:

1. The hypodermic injection of morphia.

2. The use of morphia by the mouth or rectum.

3. The use of alcoholic preparations of opium by the mouth.

4. The use of gum opium by the mouth.

5. The use of the extract of opium by inhalation (opium-smoking).

Dr. N. Allen[1] states that the lungs offer so large and so delicate an absorbing surface, and so greatly is free oxygenation of the blood interfered with, that the effects of opium-smoking must be greater than those from using the drug in any other way. It

[1] The Opium Trade, Lowell, 1853.

must be remembered, however, that at the time at
which Dr. Allen wrote, the hypodermic injection of
morphia was wholly unknown to him or to any other
physician in the United States, and but little known
in England, for Hunter was one of the first to urge
the advantages of Dr. Wood's discovery, and his
papers appeared several years later. (In the *Medical Times & Gazette*, 1858–1859, and June 3, 1865;
also "On the Speedy Relief of Pain," etc., London,
1865.) Furthermore, Dr. Allen's propositions are
lacking in facts to sustain them, as will be evident
to any medical man who reads them. He has failed
to take into account the part played by the residual
and tidal air.

As regards financial and moral ruin, opium-smoking should, unquestionably, head the list.

Longevity.—Does opium-smoking shorten life?
There is much evidence *pro* and *con.* The vice has
existed for so short a time in this country that I can
offer no original observations upon this point and
must depend entirely upon the statements of others.
Calkins [1] says :

Observers, neither few nor obscure, have raised the question
whether any curtailment of the life term is to be ascribed, of course, to
the free use of opium. Dr. O'Shaugnessy, of Calcutta, one of the
doubters, declares his opinion thus : " The longevity of the opium-
eater is proverbial." Smokers not a few, sixty and seventy years old,
who had been addicted half their lives, came under the notice of Sur-

[1] *Op. cit.*, p. 100.

geon Smith.   Dr. Oxley was assured by several [1] such that neither is life shortened nor health impaired, provided due limitations in quantity are maintained.   Dr. Burnes, at the court of Runjeet Singh, remarked that the people of that locality did not, to appearance, suffer much from using opium, nor was there any visible contraction of the natural period.   Sir John Browning, a resident in Canton in an official capacity for twenty years, pronounces the accounts published by many tourists as superficial in description and overwrought in detail.   Here at home Dr. C. A. Lee reckons it far from proven that opium, used in moderation, [2] either contracts the expected term or impairs functional regularity.

These views are strengthened, certainly, by certain known facts. Thus, Dr. Harper, at the dispensary in the fen district of Lancashire, counted up, one day, out of the entire company of consumers, fifteen persons averaging in quantity $\frac{1}{8}$ to $\frac{1}{2}$ an ounce, whose medium age was 75 years.   The Assei-Batang (gold-traders), a very industrious class, though notably given to the smoking of opium, are healthy and robust, says Marsden ; and even in the factories at Benares, the atmosphere of which is constantly charged with pulverulent particles or vapory exhalations arising from the gummy masses, the packers and other manipulators have an average of life comparing favorably with the handicraft workers generally (Eatwell).

Reports and opinions in discrepancy with such are not wanting, however.   Dr. Oxley, while resident in Singapore, had never met (a single instance, an octogenarian, excepted) the first opium-eater that had gone beyond maturity.   Dr. Madden, at the Constantinople Bazaar, found but one visitor who had passed his climacteric, a man who had formed the habit twenty-five years before.   Most of the thériakis present were apparently short of thirty-five. [3]   Dr. Parker

---

[1] This statement is worthless, owing to the well-known fact that an opium-taker will invariably lie about his habit.

[2] There are so few who use it in moderation that this statement is without value.

[3] Shortening of the life period in *opium-eaters* is not the question under consideration, and testimony to that effect can be of value only indirectly.   From it we would *suppose* that *opium-smoking* would shorten life, but actual proof of the fact is lacking, and reliable statistics can never be obtained until we have

and Dr. Macgowan, both, after an extended survey of the field, express corresponding views. Says De Ponqueville, "The man who begins at twenty cannot expect to pass his thirty-sixth year" (a point twenty-five years short of his term, according to the life tables), and Oppenheim concurs. Pohlman, American missionary at Amoy, and Martin, of the Civil Service, would reduce even this term. Dr. Little, a final appellant in all inquiries that pertain to opium, affirms that the stimulus, when freely used, not only shortens the term of life, but operates powerfully in making that life miserable so long as it lasts. American physicians hold similar views. Dr. Palmer had but three patients, at most, who had neared seventy ; most fell short of the meridian.

Thus speaks Cabanis upon narcotic stimuli in general : "L'usage habituelle de narcotiques contribue beaucoup à la longue à hâter vieillesse précoce, énervant avant le temps, et s'aggravant de jour au our." Of twenty-nine dètenus at the House of Correction in Singapore, all Chinamen, the twenty-one who smoked, bore, every one of them, a sickly aspect, with indications of premature decline ; of the nine besides, only two had been invalids in any respect.

---

exact Chinese death and sanitary reports, and it will be many years before these, are obtainable. Furthermore, famine, poverty, excessive sexual indulgence, gambling, lack of all sanitary measures, personal and general, and the like, enter as factors into this very complex problem.

If solitary or a few examples of shortened life term amongst opium-eaters are to be taken as evidence against long life amongst opium-smokers, examples quite as numerous can be brought forward to prove longevity amongst eaters. As follows: " Longevity in the prospective is to be determined not upon the citation of instances, exclusively, but from *physical condition and social surroundings* (italics mine) also. Plato died in harness, as it were, that is, pen in hand, at the ripe age of 84. Suleyman, of Constantinople, passed into his 99th year. Dr. Burnes cites the case of Visrajée, a Cutchee chief, 80 years old, and more, at the time, with health unimpaired, though an eater a lifetime. Schlegel's woman lived upon laudanum, one might say, having used it regularly from her 49th to her 70th year, and at the rate of 300 drops in her last years. Dr. Christison instances a woman of 70, who had been habituated 40 years of the time ; and another, a Leith woman, who used half an ounce as long and lived ten years longer. Dr. Pidduck had a similar case of the other sex. A Brooklyn pharmaceutist furnishes for this record the case of a grandmother, who died at 98, having, in a measure, subsisted upon laudanum for a quarter of her life, etc., etc., etc. (Calkins)." Parrish, Golding Bird, and many others have known similar cases. I, myself, can cite at least twenty, some of whom are still living.

It would be very interesting to have full and exact statistics upon the question of longevity as affected by opium-taking and smoking; but they are not ob-

Koo-Kinshan claims[1] that life is decidedly short-ened by the use of the pipe. The worthlessness, however, of the evidence of the Chinese upon any thing medical may be judged from the following taken from the same author:

9. *It attacks the vitals.* By a long continuance of the habit worms are generated in the abdomen,[2] and in the confirmed smokers the baneful influences attack the intestines, and great injury is the conse-quence,—injury which the most celebrated physicians can never avert.

He then bases his argument as to the harm done, by continued use, on the symptoms and *post-mortem* appearances that are found in cases of acute poison-ing, etc., which is wholly without justification. He then continues:

Once, when on a journey, it happened that a fellow-passenger, who was a smoker, had used up all his opium. The periodical desire for it came on, and finding no means to gratify his appetite, he strove to take away his own life. By mistake he swallowed a cup of oil, which induced excessive vomiting, when he threw up a collection of noxious worms, parti-colored, with red heads, and hairy. They crawled upon the ground to the great astonishment of the spectators.

tainable at present. We can only say from *a priori* reasoning that it is *probable* that the natural term of life is abridged somewhat, if the drug is used to de-cided excess. To ascribe the early death of *every* opium-smoker to opium, as has been done, is, however, unjustifiable and nonsensical.

[1] Foreign Opium a Poison ; illustrated in ten paragraphs by Koo-Kinshan. Chinese Repository, vol. vii, p. 109.

[2] This is true, in a measure, for there is usually a condition of gastric and intestinal catarrh produced by prolonged smoking, and, being accompanied by an excessive secretion of mucus, produces a condition favorable to the existence of both the ascaris and the thread-worm. Exception is, of course, taken to the word " generated."

No mention is made of what became of the man. A mind that will patch together, as cause and effect, the habitual use of opium and the vomiting of some lumbricoids, is a very poor one to arrive at any definite and reliable conclusions as to how the drug affects the tissue or function of any of the vital organs.

Surgeon Smith, of Pulo-Penang, as also S. Wells Williams, take a fairer view of longevity as affected by opium-smoking, when the first says[1] that it is the poor, who are in no position to live well, whose term of life is abridged ; while the rich, whose sanitary surroundings, care of the person, and a full diet are not materially affected, as regards this point, at least.   And the last :[2]

> There has not yet been opportunity to make those minute investigations respecting the extent opium is used amongst the Chinese, what classes of people use it, their daily dose, the proportion of reprobate smokers, and many other points which have been narrowly examined into in regard to the use of alcohol, etc. (p. 394).   The disastrous effects of the drug upon the constitution seem to be somewhat delayed or modified by the quantity of nourishing food the person can procure, and consequently it is among the poor, who can least afford the pipe, and still less the injury done their energies, that the destruction of life is the greatest.

I propose to briefly review here the more remote effects of this vice on the individual and the nation.

---

[1] Chinese Repository, Nov., 1842.
[2] The Middle Kingdom, vol. ii, p. 391.

The prowess of a people must of necessity be influenced decidedly by a vice that affects so many of its number. This is the more so when the individuals addicted to the practice are not herded together in one part of the country, but are spread over a large part, indeed the whole of the empire, for then, by association and intermarriage, the spread of the vice and the perpetuation of its ill effects, though less marked in point of intensity, more directly affect the people as a whole. If the practice was confined to the inhabitants of a single district in China, the study of the habit both as regards the individual and his offspring would be less difficult, and it would be more easy to control or wholly do away with it by laws properly enforced. When, however, it is prevalent amongst all classes, and throughout all parts of the country, its effect upon the nation is much more decided, and its suppression more questionable, for the very functionaries to whom the carrying out of the laws is entrusted are found to be themselves confirmed habitués, who are loth to take any decided step against their own weakness.

So thickly settled is China, so inadequate are the means of transportation, so poor are the majority of its inhabitants, that flood, crop-failures, or fire, result in almost every instance in the most terrible famine and suffering. Occurrences that would in no way affect the welfare of the people in this country or

England, such as a prolonged drought, are, when occurring in China or India, of the greatest moment, resulting usually in death by starvation, not of a few, but of thousands, both rich and poor.

Hence, it will be seen that every acre of ground available for the raising of cereals or vegetables is absolutely required in order to avoid disastrous results. Of late years the poppy has been planted in whole districts, crowding out the cultivation of those things necessary for food. To be sure, these growers receive more money for their opium than they would for their corn or rice, but if famine comes, the question is not one of money at all, for the inadequate means of transportation permit the death of thousands before the money-bought provisions can reach them from other provinces. Take the following as an example. In speaking of the terrible famine and the terrible suffering of the people in Northern China in 1877 or '78, Mr. David H. Bailey, United States Consul-General at Shanghai, says:[1]

In attempting to give a cause for this famine, I must unquestionably state it to be the failure of the cereal and vegetable crops arising from drought in the provinces which have suffered. But to the political economist who might interest himself in the matter, other indirect reasons might not unlikely arise,—the significant fact that in the inland provinces of China the poppy plant has, more and more of late years, been cultivated to the neglect of cereals, and upon the

---

[1] U. S. Consular Reports on Trade, Commerce, etc., vol. xviii, p. 227.

very ground where grain was formerly grown. Such provinces, therefore, as Shanshi, Hoonan, and Shense, where the famine has been
worst, yearly become more dependent upon outside sources for their
food supplies, and when the local grain crop failed, both private and
government means of transportation were found to be insufficient to
bring in the required means of subsistence, and the rich and poor
starved alike.

It may be said that if the opium trade was legal-
ized, etc., that the poppy would not have been as
extensively grown in China, and hence the famine
would not have occurred. But it must be remembered that drought and famine are not unusual in
India, and from the same cause, and that the de-
bauchery of the Chinese with English or any other
opium, would produce a condition of lethargy that
would make the efficient working and storing of any
crop other than that of the poppy, which pandered
to the popular vice, a very debatable question.

The condition of mental and bodily hebetude that
is certain to follow the excessive use of this drug by
the pipe must, of necessity, cause present and future
physical weakness and deterioration that can only
result in national decay. The religion of a people,
however crude and untruthful, tends to keep that
people within certain moral bounds. The Chinese
priesthood are addicted to the pipe, and the people
forget to perform the religious rites. The "opium
pistol" (*yen tsiang*) is their God, the opium extract
their heaven. Moreover, the true Christian relig-

ion, the real civilizer of all nations, meets a double difficulty,—the apathy of the opium-soaked habitué, and the ill example of a Christian nation forcing a vice upon another.

The stability and prosperity of a nation depend largely upon its agricultural classes. This is more truthful with regard to China than almost any other nation in the world, for the prolonged isolation of the country from all others, and the scarcity of food, with the large dependence upon cereals and vegetables, and the necessity of home culture to avoid actual starvation, have justly raised this class to a high standing in the community.[1] To-day, legitimate husbandry is giving way, in all parts of the country, with great rapidity to the cultivation of the poppy, and the agriculturists are themselves becoming addicted to the use of the baneful drug that will mentally and physically unfit them for work and ruin them financially.

The stability and prosperity of a nation are in a great measure dependent on its army, and the efficiency of the army on the courage and physical development of its soldiers and the integrity and knowledge of its officers. Calkins[2] says:

---

[1] Williams says : (p. 100) " Agriculture holds the first place, in their estimation, among the branches of labor, and the honors paid to it by the annual ploughing ceremony are given from a deep sense of its importance to the public welfare." The annual ceremony of ploughing, here referred to, consists in the ploughing of a certain number of furrows, each in a sacred field, by the emperor, princes, and ministers.

[2] *Op. cit.*, p. 147.

Among the Orientals opium is used as a preparative for the bat-tle-field. In 1850 (Chinese Register) just as a fight with the rebel forces on the northern frontier was impending, it was found one morning that the imperial soldiery, to the number of some thousands, had made a stampede for a foray upon the neighboring country, with the intent of renewing their stock of opium. What precise advantage, however, is to be expected from such stimulus may be calculated by the fact mentioned by Huc in relation to the campaign of 1832 against the Yaous, that the emperor's army, though numerically superior, fell much below their adversaries in pluck and steadiness. The repeated successes secured by the rebel chief, often against great odds, are ascribed by this tourist to the abjuration of opium, as exacted by them in accordance with the prescribed rule of military service.

With some other peoples, however, as the Turks, he claims that their bravery is materially assisted by the use of opium. A man who fights for a good cause needs no urging, and the bravery built on stimulants is as ineffective as it is ephemeral.

In the Chinese Repository for May, 1832, we find the following significant paragraph : " Of 1000 men sent by the Governor of Canton to act against the rebels, the commanding officer sent back 200 as rendered totally unfit for active service by the habit of opium-smoking."

The navy, too, such as it is, must be demoralized. The sailors were amongst the first to obtain and use the drug. Furthermore, pirates and smugglers swarm along the whole coast, endeavoring to evade the laws, and preying upon the ships of all nations,

thus materially affecting the commerce of other nations with this country.

The prosperity of a country largely depends upon
its statesmen, scholars, and magistracy. Laws
must not only be wisely made but must be effi-
ciently enforced. It is said that the late emperor
was a smoker, and it is a well-known fact that despite the most stringent laws against smuggling and
smoking, the traffic and the vice have been in no way
curtailed, owing to the very insufficiency, and de-
ceit, and bribe-taking of those persons in whose
hands the carrying out of it, was placed. No man
who smokes opium is fit to make laws, administer
justice, or consider rationally subjects that involve
the welfare of a nation.

" In China," says Calkins, " the habit was originally confined to the belted gentry, gentlemen of
fortune, and other exclusives proper; but in progress, tradesmen, artisans, laborers, and then priests
and women soon caught the infection, until finally
all distinctions determined by caste or condition
were obliterated."

" First to break over the interdicts as decreed by
the imperial authority was the very class, who, from
their social position, should have been foremost in
good example, the mandarins."

The future of a people depends upon the mental,
physical, and moral condition of its children, and

the children must of necessity suffer from the vices
or profit by the virtues of their progenitors. A nation of opium-smokers cannot beget healthy children ; nor will their deteriorated offspring profit by
the prevalent vices or the evil example of their parents. For instance : " When Vasco da Gama and Al-
buquerque voyaged to Malacca, there to plant colo-
nies that should reflect lustre upon their ancient
mother, little prescience had they, even in dim
shadow, of the debasement and the apathy into
which these settlements were eventually to sink.
' Here upon this Peninsula,' says Dr. Yvan, ' where the
Portuguese settlers number at most but three thousand, one may see on every street boys with etio-
lated complexion and puny limb, who if perchance
they survive the period of childhood will pass at
once to that of adult life (for here there is no intervening season of youth), to lapse ere long into a
premature decrepitude. An enemy, subtle as the
serpent, more malignant than war and pestilence
combined, has wrought out the mischief. So, too,
Formosa (Isle of Beauty) presents the spectacle of
a race once hardy and warlike, but now sunken in
an emasculating decline through subjection to the
same pestilent invader.' Of the children in Malacca
whose parents have been habituated to opium, says
Surgeon Smith : ' They go about with the physical
expression of general enervation, and in their

mental aspect the imprint of dulness and fatuity. So of the boys in Amoy, whose index-marks are watery eyes, sunken cheeks, and sallow faces, an idiotic expression, and a mopy gait.' Verily, 'the iniquities of the fathers are visited upon the children even unto the third and fourth generations.' "— (Calkins.)

This, however, is not direct evidence. We have none such at present. With opium- and morphia-taking, impotence in the male and sterility in the female almost certainly follow. In opium-smokers the impression upon the sexual and generative function is not so well marked, as will be seen by reference to a previous chapter (Chap. vi). This, at least, is the case amongst American smokers. It is a question, however, whether the same holds true with regard to the Chinese who, as a rule, are sexually exhausted, or rather impaired, at an early age from excesses. Statistics would go to show that the number of children born is materially affected by this vice. Certain conclusions, however, cannot be drawn until more exact knowledge is had of the part played by famine and wars, and the nature and mortality of the diseases most prevalent are better understood. It is even a question whether the various census returns from which we draw our conclusions are correct, for the enumeration was often made for the purpose of levying a poll-tax ; and it

was to the interest of the census-taker, if dishonest,—
and Chinese officials are notably so,—to make a
smaller return than was correct and pocket the
balance, and of the individual not to be included,
and avoid taxation.

The pathological effects of opium-smoking have
been spoken of already and its effects upon the
individual and the nation have been shown in this
chapter. My wish is not to underestimate the baneful influence of this manner of using the drug upon
the system, but to weed out such errors as have
from loose statements and inference been heretofore published, and to thus put the question upon
a firm basis of truth, for nothing is ever gained, I
am firmly convinced, from exaggerating the true
facts for the purpose of more efficient popular agita-
tion. Viewed from any stand-point the practice is
filthy and disgusting ; is a reef that is bound to sink
morality ; is a curse to the parent, the child,
and the government ; is a fertile cause of crime,
lying, insanity, debt, and suicide ; is a poison to
hope and ambition ; a sunderer of family ties ; a
breeder of sensuality and, finally, impotence ; a destroyer of bodily and mental function ; and a thing
to be viewed with abhorence by every honest man
and virtuous woman.

Some authors have attempted to excuse the vice
of opium-smoking on the ground that it is less in-

jurious than spirit-drinking. Alcohol enters directly into the composition of the tissues, and when
used to excess, produces organic lesions of the
viscera that usually have a fatal termination.
Opium, on the contrary, rarely causes organic
change, its force being expended in variously
modifying, disordering, or stopping function. The
opium-smoker does not beat his wife, break his
furniture, stab his friends, shoot his enemy, insult
the passer-by, or scatter his money broadcast while
under the influence of the drug, as does the drunkard.
Nor does he go reeling through the streets, a dis-
grace to himself and his friends, and wind up his
debauch, comatose, in the gutter. I do not question
but that if 15,000,000 Chinamen were daily befud-
dling their brains and ruining their bodies with
liquor, the ill effects upon the individual and the
nation would be as great and even greater than those
arising from opium-smoking.

This, however, cannot be offered as an excuse for
England's course, or in extenuation of the prevail-
ing vice. Because robbery is less of a crime than
murder, the perpetration of the former is not justi-
fied by that fact, nor could the individual who furnished the robber with the pick-lock and jimmy,
urge in extenuation that he might have given him a
revolver and a poignard.

MEASURES FOR REFORM.

1. The first step, and one that common decency and humanity, aside from every other consideration, demands, is the withdrawal of the English from the opium traffic with China, an international agreement to be signed by the representatives of all peoples to supply no opium to the Chinese market.

2. Circulars translated into the Chinese language stating that fact, showing the evil effects of the vice in all parts of the world, and offering free cure to all who wish to avail themselves of the opportunity, should be printed and spread broadcast over China; and

3. The establishment, in various parts of the empire, of small, well-appointed hospitals for the treatment of the habit. Such hospitals under the care of medical men of ability would be inexpensive and would undoubtedly do a world of good; for, by the free use of baths, electricity, and the proper remedies, a rapid cure could be accomplished.

Moreover, the statistics thus obtainable would fully repay the outlay. The Chinese government would, undoubtedly, bear a part of the expense of these hospitals.

The present system of occasional devotion of a part of a general missionary hospital to the treatment of this habit is any thing but satisfactory, although very commendable in view of need of some help for the victims.

The opium-smoking habit, contrary to the general relief, when undertaken on scientific principles, can be rapidly, painlessly, and safely cured. With those whom I have cured I have experienced but very little trouble, and have never had one in my Home for more than one week. All the the symptoms heretofore considered dangerous and distressing can now be easily and effectually met, nay, even anticipated.

The ease with which this habit can be cured, as compared with the suffering felt by the ordinary opium-eater or morphia-injector, is, to my mind, one of the strongest proofs that this is less of a habit, and less injurious, physically, than any other manner of using the drug.

I have not treated enough cases yet, and a sufficient time since cure has not elapsed to permit me to speak definitely regarding the relative frequency of relapses.

SOCIAL PROBLEMS
AND
SOCIAL POLICY:
The American Experience

An Arno Press Collection

Bachman, George W. and Lewis Meriam. **The Issue of Compulsory Health Insurance.** 1948

Bishop, Ernest S. **The Narcotic Drug Problem.** 1920

Bosworth, Louise Marion. **The Living Wage of Women Workers.** 1911

[Brace, Emma, editor]. **The Life of Charles Loring Brace.** 1894

Brown, Esther Lucile. **Social Work as a Profession.** 4th Edition. 1942

Brown, Roy M. **Public Poor Relief in North Carolina.** 1928

Browning, Grace. **Rural Public Welfare.** 1941

Bruce, Isabel Campbell and Edith Eickhoff. **The Michigan Poor Law.** 1936

Burns, Eveline M. **Social Security and Public Policy.** 1956

Cahn, Frances and Valeska Bary. **Welfare Activities of Federal, State, and Local Governments in California, 1850-1934.** 1936

Campbell, Persia. **The Consumer Interest.** 1949

Davies, Stanley Powell. **Social Control of the Mentally Deficient.** 1930

Devine, Edward T. **The Spirit of Social Work.** 1911

Douglas, Paul H. and Aaron Director. **The Problem of Unemployment.** 1931

Eaton, Allen in Collaboration with Shelby M. Harrison. **A Bibliography of Social Surveys.** 1930

Epstein, Abraham. **The Challenge of the Aged.** 1928

Falk, I[sidore] S., Margaret C. Klem, and Nathan Sinai. **The Incidence of Illness and the Receipt and Costs of Medical Care Among Representative Families.** 1933

Fisher, Irving. **National Vitality, its Wastes and Conservation.** 1909

Freund, Ernst. **The Police Power:** Public Policy and Constitutional Rights. 1904

Gladden, Washington. **Applied Christianity:** Moral Aspects of Social Questions. 1886

Hartley, Isaac Smithson, editor. **Memorial of Robert Milham Hartley.** 1882

Hollander, Jacob H. **The Abolition of Poverty.** 1914

Kane, H[arry] H[ubbell]. **Opium-Smoking in America and China.** 1882

Klebaner, Benjamin Joseph. **Public Poor Relief in America, 1790-1860.** 1951

Knapp, Samuel L. **The Life of Thomas Eddy.** 1834

Lawrence, Charles. **History of the Philadelphia Almshouses and Hospitals from the Beginning of the Eighteenth to the Ending of the Nineteenth Centuries.** 1905

[Massachusetts Commission on the Cost of Living]. **Report of the Commission on the Cost of Living.** 1910

[Massachusetts Commission on Old Age Pensions, Annuities and Insurance]. **Report of the Commission on Old Age Pensions, Annuities and Insurance.** 1910

[New York State Commission to Investigate Provision for the Mentally Deficient]. **Report of the State Commission to Investigate Provision for the Mentally Deficient.** 1915

[Parker, Florence E., Estelle M. Stewart, and Mary Conymgton, compilers]. **Care of Aged Persons in the United States.** 1929

Pollock, Horatio M., editor. **Family Care of Mental Patients.** 1936

Pollock, Horatio M. **Mental Disease and Social Welfare.** 1941

Powell, Aaron M., editor. **The National Purity Congress;** Its Papers, Addresses, Portraits. 1896

The President's Commission on the Health Needs of the Nation. **Building America's Health.** [1952]. Five vols. in two

Prostitution in America: Three Investigations, 1902-1914. 1975

Rubinow, I[saac] M. **The Quest for Security.** 1934

Shaffer, Alice, Mary Wysor Keefer, and Sophonisba P. Breckinridge. **The Indiana Poor Law.** 1936

Shattuck, Lemuel. **Report to the Committee of the City Council Appointed to Obtain the Census of Boston for the Year 1845.** 1846

The State and Public Welfare in Nineteenth-Century America: Five Investigations, 1833-1877. 1975

Stewart, Estelle M. **The Cost of American Almshouses.** 1925

Taylor, Graham. **Pioneering on Social Frontiers.** 1930

[United States Senate Committee on Education and Labor]. **Report of the Committee of the Senate Upon the Relations Between Labor and Capital.** 1885. Four vols.

Walton, Robert P. **Marihuana, America's New Drug Problem.** 1938

Williams, Edward Huntington. **Opiate Addiction.** 1922

Williams, Pierce assisted by Isabel C. Chamberlain. **The Purchase of Medical Care Through Fixed Periodic Payment.** 1932

Willoughby, W[estal] W[oodbury]. **Opium as an International Problem.** 1925

Wisner, Elizabeth. **Public Welfare Administration in Louisiana.** 1930